HEXING
the
PATRIARCHY

HEXING
the
PATRIARCHY

**26 Potions, Spells, and Magical Elixirs
to Embolden the Resistance**

ARIEL GORE

SEAL PRESS

NEW YORK

Advance Praise for

HEXING THE PATRIARCHY

"Ariel Gore's magical, majestic *Hexing the Patriarchy* is a field guide to fixing what's wrong with the world. . . . Just holding this book in my hands made me feel giddy with hope."
  —**KAREN KARBO**, author of *In Praise of Difficult Women*

"We have needed this book for centuries! Ariel Gore, in all her witchy-smart goodness, will inspire you, bolster you, lift you up, remind you who you are, and show you how to find your power in a world that is constantly trying to keep you from having it."
  —**KERRY COHEN**, author of *Lush and Loose Girl*

"It's time to conjure. Ariel Gore's *Hexing the Patriarchy* is a call to arms . . . a magical field guide that will set the crap that needs to burn on fire."
  —**LIDIA YUKNAVITCH**

"Ariel Gore has given us . . . the tools and the nerve to be magic."
  —**SOPHIA SHALMIYEV**, author of *Mother Winter*

"This alphabetized witch primer had me at 'B: binding spells for grabby assholes'!"
  —**JENNIFER BAUMGARDNER**

"I endorse Ariel Gore's book, which covers everything from wholesome light witchcraft for health to what you gotta do to punch your enemy in the throat."
  —**JENNIFER BLOWDRYER**,
    journalist and punk music artist

For

MAIA & MAX

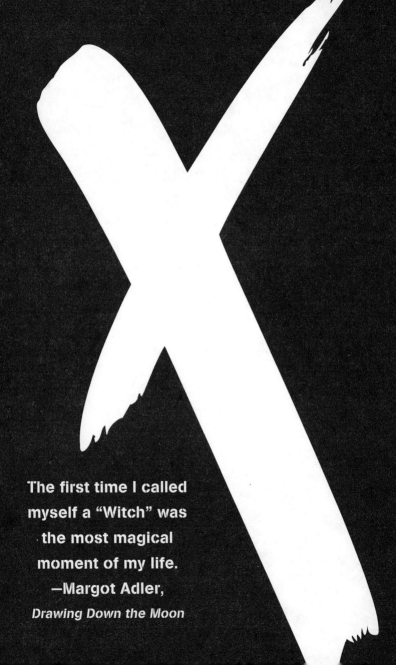

The first time I called
myself a "Witch" was
the most magical
moment of my life.
—Margot Adler,
Drawing Down the Moon

CONTENTS

INTRODUCTION:

MAGICAL LETTERS

I formally initiated myself as a witch when I was a twenty-one-year-old single mom surviving on welfare and student loans. The patriarchy had me by the throat in the form of misogynist family court judges, food-stamp-cutting governors, and national politicians happy to dehumanize poor women to feed their own greed for power. I felt like I was under legislative, financial, and psychic attack all at once—because I was.

I'd been talking to owls since before I could talk to people, and now, in an acquaintance's forested backyard, I came upon a deer. When we locked eyes, I decided she was a messenger of the Goddess, and I whispered a little prayer: *We're up shit creek here. Send help if you can.*

The very next day, in an old-school brick-and-mortar bookstore that smelled of coffee and wet leaves, I happened upon a copy of *Witchcraft for Tomorrow* by the British witch Doreen Valiente. I read "The Witch's Ballad" on the first page, and I thought, *Count me the fuck in.*

I followed Doreen's instructions for self-initiation, and I made a plan: I would magically defend myself from the patriarchy, and once I'd recovered my strength, I'd go on the offensive.

I lived in Sonoma County, California—kind of Witchville central at the time—and soon enough, I found a few witchy elders to help me on my way.

One of the first assignments I got from one of those witchy elders was to create my own alphabet.

"My own alphabet?" I felt a deliciously childish *ting!* in my chest at the idea. "Like the secret codes I used to make when I was a kid?"

My elder took a drag from her menthol cigarette, grabbed a handful of tortilla chips, and laughed. "*Just* like that, honey."

Creating my own secret alphabet, painstaking and fanciful—I mean, how *do* you decide what your W will look like?—came as excellent relief from the daily work of mothering and adulting in a world that hated mothers and only seemed to value adults as consumers. Maybe my O would look like my baby's satisfied belly. My Z could be a lightning bolt to zap feminist sense into the people who had power over me. My I would be a raised revolutionary fist with a great blood-red manicure.

My toddler daughter was learning her English ABCs at the same time, so we sat in our sunny dining nook, learning to spell and write spells together, and everything smelled of oranges.

I was in college then, too, and working nights with my Chinese professor on an ambitious English translation of Nushu, the secret written language used exclusively by women in nineteenth- and twentieth-century Southern China when women were excluded from male literacy. Nushu script was phonetic, unlike the written patriarchal Chinese I'd been studying since I was a kid, and passed down from mother to daughter. Rural and working-class women used Nushu to write and embroider songs, poems, oracles, spells, gossip, and congratulations and condolences after weddings.

> Beside a well,
> one does not thirst.
> Beside a sister,
> one does not despair.
> —NUSHU SAYING

The *China Daily* called Yang Huanyi, the last living woman who'd grown up using Nushu, "the oldest inheritress of . . . probably the world's only female-specific language." But now it occurred to me that women and poor people had always created their own alphabets and their own languages when the languages of their fathers or those in power were turned against them—or forbidden altogether.

It made sense to start with an alphabet. I would soon learn to spell out spells. I'd curse the family court judges in cursive. I'd write a new future beyond these dehumanizing systems I'd been trained to blame myself for getting snared in.

Yang Huanyi died in 2004.

Only scholars know her matrilineal language now.

But I refuse to believe that only tender and good things can vanish.

Instead, let's vanquish racism, misogyny, capitalism, xenophobia, homophobia, transphobia, and exploitation on scales both micro and monstrous.

The patriarchs in power want us to believe that "boys will be boys," and racist dog whistles are legitimate campaign platforms, and unequal pay has some nonbigoted "logical" explanation. But we see through that gaslighting bullshit.

We're spelling out our resistance.

Since my first initiation back in Sonoma County, I've practiced magic in a handful of distinct traditions—from Wicca to Spiritualism and, when expressly invited, Santería and Voodoo. None of these traditions asked me to renounce the others, so I didn't. Some asked me not to talk about them too much, so I won't. But the basic path—whether we're formally initiated or not—has always been about uncovering our inherent divinity and stepping into our spiritual authority. And my first teacher for *that* was the Catholic priest who would become my stepfather.

I first met Father John when I was four years old.

He had a Black Panther poster taped to one wall of his office, a print that announced "The Spirit of the Lord is Freedom" on another, and a picture of a Sierra mountain taped to his desk. I would grow up to understand that my dad believed in this trinity completely: political activism to heal us all from the dehumanization of white supremacy plus a spirituality that was all about freedom plus an anchoring in the natural world equals good hope for liberation.

He was, not surprisingly, excommunicated from the Catholic Church on the very day he became my stepfather.

I thought that was a shady move on the church's part, but my newly unemployed stepfather seemed unfazed. He just rolled a thin piece of paper into his typewriter and responded to the archbishop's excommunication letter—a document that forbade him from so much as receiving Holy Communion in the institution he'd served his entire adult life—by telling the archbishop that his decree sounded like something out of the Inquisition.

"Despite the hollow booming of your Automatic Canons," my stepfather wrote, "I am peacefully in communion with the universal Church and shall receive communion when I please."

Now the Catholic kids of the nonliberation variety weren't allowed to play with me anymore, but I took my cue from my stepfather and shrugged off their rigidity like they were *so yesterday.* I was introverted, anyway, so I appreciated my unearned pass from the dreadful social scene that was the Early Birds Kindergarten Group at Addison Elementary. Instead, I spent my afternoons making collages out of psalms in my stepfather's wood-floored office: yes, we lived in a world made of spiritual words, and we were free to rearrange them as we pleased.

Along with being born into Catholicism and achieving that priesthood as a young man, my stepfather grew up with

American Spiritualist séances, and now he carried his old family ouija board up the concrete stairs from the basement and we all asked the spirits to become our life coaches.

In the early twentieth century, when my stepfather was a kid, Spiritualism was still a major religious movement and not seen as being in conflict with Catholicism or any other tradition.

My stepfather believed that his dead aunt Mina joined us for dinner every evening at seven. We always set a place for her. In the 1980s, he rewrote his Bible, using female pronouns for God. He ordained a witch. He performed weddings for queer and trans Catholics. And soon, he taught me to move physical matter.

I shit you not. When my stepfather forgot his glasses on his way to his job as a bookseller at Printer's Ink Bookstore, he didn't have to turn his old three-speed bike around and come home. He just pulled over to the curb, closed his eyes, and concentrated on moving the glasses through time and space. When he felt done with his task, he opened his eyes, reached into his pocket and—four times out of five—found his glasses there.

I thought this was an excellent trick. I wanted to know how to do it, too! John explained his process simply, like the ability to move objects with his mind was quite everyday and just a matter of practice. He told me to close my eyes and visualize in absolutely vivid detail the item I wanted to move, beginning by picturing it in its likely current location and moving it slowly—visualizing as many turns as I needed it to take—and then placing it someplace where it could *possibly* be anyway. Magic like this, I understood from his explanation, did not like to make a "provable" spectacle of itself.

I trained in this process daily, focusing my energy on moving money from the Great Western Bank up on Hamilton Avenue into the pages of the Alice in Wonderland books on my bottom shelf. I didn't think of this practice as psychic bank robbery, but I guess that's what it was. In any case, I became quite adept at it. I started with small amounts of money and eventually could move ten dollar bills with confidence.

I know. You want to know if I can still do it. But a witch has to have some secrets.

My Gammie Evelyn, an old-school Hollywood dame, had her own way of dialoguing with what she couldn't see. Each morning, she psychically scanned her body for health issues, and then she meditated through them. She learned this technique from her own grandmother, who we all called Aunt Eva, a widowed Christian Science practitioner and single mom who came out to California in the early 1900s with my young great-grandmother, Miss Nellie Mae. (Christian Science is the medicine-adverse religion founded by the spiritual medium Mary Baker Eddy in the late 1800s—nothing to do with Scientology.)

My Gammie Evelyn had left the church by the time I knew her, but she still did her daily health meditations. She drank like a fish, drove a red Cadillac, never went to the doctor, lived until she was ninety-one, and donated her body to medical research as an example of an undoctored woman.

It turns out that my stepfather's family's work with their ouija board and my Gammie Evelyn's health meditations were both related to modern Spiritualism, a distinct religion and a broader religious movement that at times sure looks a lot like a way of rebranding witchcraft so as not to get us burned. At its peak at the turn of the twentieth century, there were some ten million Spiritualists in the United States and England. It was a major religion—not considered fringe or esoteric.

Some Spiritualists were Christians and some weren't—either way, feminism, the abolition of slavery, and antiracism were intrinsic tenets of the religion.

Progressive politics and the spirit world were good friends.

Years later I would learn that Doreen Valiente, the author of *Witchcraft for Tomorrow*—that book I'd happened upon back in Sonoma County—belonged to a Spiritualist church for a while herself. In *I Am a Witch*, she wrote: "If I say that witches have links with Spiritualism, this will probably upset some Spiritualists; but it is nevertheless true. In fact, every genuine phenomenon connected with modern Spiritualism can be found occurring in ancient witchcraft; mediumship, clairvoyance and clairaudience, psychic healing, levitation, astral projection, materialisations, even the formation of the circle by placing men and women alternately to balance the power."

Doreen was, like me, a high school dropout with grand aspirations. But she was more badass. In her late teens, she used her deep understanding of language and letters to become a translator at Bletchley Park, the hub for codebreaking against the Nazis. She was a pro-choice spy and a legit psychic who in the early 1950s obtained some original notebooks delineating the magical system of the Hermetic Order of the Golden Dawn, a secret society whose founding members included W. B. Yeats.

In 1953, two years after Britain repealed the laws banning witchcraft, Doreen was initiated by Gerald Gardner, another influential witch for whom she often served as a ghostwriter. Her instructions for self-initiation in *Witchcraft for Tomorrow* are, to my knowledge, the first ever published.

When my daughter and I moved from Sonoma County to Oakland in the early 1990s, the witchy folks we met worked primarily in Ifa, Santería, Voodoo, and Conjure—all based in African traditional religions. I was familiar with the magic in Luisah Teish's 1985 Voodoo primer *Jambalaya: The Natural Woman's*

Book of Personal Charms and Practical Rituals—hell, my sister and her friend had practically burned down our mother's studio trying to evoke the orisha Elegua that year—and my new friends invited me to participate further, saying, "Good, Teish's book was orisha kindergarten. We're going to move you into orisha elementary school." And in orisha elementary I began to learn new avenues to connect with the unseen world.

Magic, I was learning, wasn't just about influencing our physical realities but also about retrieving the energy the patriarchy has taken from us. I felt happy: here were adaptable, urban, ancestor- and earth-based spiritual systems that had forged web-like paths to our West Coast community. Originating in Yoruban West Africa, Voudoun practitioners syncretized their religion with Catholicism and other Christian sects as a way to preserve it without getting punished by their enslavers. Voudoun also fomented with pagan influence in the Caribbean where about eighty thousand Irish witches sold as slaves to the West Indies joined the more than three million Africans there and brought the May Pole and Madame Brigit to Voudoun. The religion arrived on the Gulf Coast before the Louisiana Purchase and soon became Voodoo, a distinct North American tradition.

If Doreen Valiente is "the Mother of Modern Witchcraft" as she has become known, Marie Laveau is the grand matriarch. One of the most important Americans of the nineteenth century, she should be in our history books with Abe Lincoln and Susan B. Anthony. But of course, she isn't—yet. I added Marie

Laveau's portrait to my dresser-top altar to remember and honor her, made the pilgrimage to her grave in New Orleans, and studied her biographies.

Born a mixed-race, "illegitimate" free woman of color in French New Orleans in 1794, the border crossed Marie Laveau, making her a US American after the Louisiana Purchase in 1803.

She was a hairdresser, a Catholic, a Mambo, a hustler, a dancer, an antislavery and prison activist, a healer and a hexer, and a powerful Voodoo queen—a Black woman who held real authority in a time when people of color and women didn't come by actionable authority easily. She knew all the secrets of the powerful white people in town, making her invulnerable to the law.

Music historian Michael Ventura considers her the mother of jazz, and hence the mother of all American music. When Marie Laveau died in 1881, she was important enough to mainstream American culture that her obituary ran in the *New York Times*. But her life story touched on everything I'd never been taught about American history, including this: magical traditions like witchcraft, Conjure, Voodoo, Hoodoo, *brujería*, Spiritualism, spiritual mediumship, Wicca, and Reclaiming have always been powerful—and female-led—religious and political forces in North America.

In 2000, my daughter and I migrated again, this time north to Portland, Oregon, and there we met traditionally trained witches and conjurers who worked with the northern mysteries—the indigenous spiritual tradition of ancient northern Europeans preserved in runic artifacts—and others who engaged in more experimental magic without formal training. I started a church with some pals—Big Mama's Church of Christ the Girlie-Man, if you must know. Our chapel was the local feminist bookstore In Other Words.

I remember a lot of communion wine.

But it made sense that a bookstore became my church. Where there is a bookstore, there is magic. A bookstore was where my stepfather found work after the Catholic Church canned him. A bookstore was where I found Doreen Valiente. A bookstore is where a writer like me sells her wares.

Over the years, wherever I lived—and especially in less-social years—writing had become my go-to conjure method. From alphabets and the void of my dreams came words and intentions and stories. With daily work and lucky manifestation, I turned my devalued labor into scrappy and beautiful books. Other writers began to send me little effigies of their own book ideas, and I put them on my altar and I did what I could to envision them into existence.

All the magical traditions I have come into contact with and made up for myself share this belief: independent of a priest, archbishop, or any formal church structure, all humans can speak to and work with hidden worlds, but we have to speak the languages of those hidden worlds, and the languages of those hidden worlds are music, word, and symbolism.

Tradition—or the use of the symbolic languages of our ancestors—amplifies power. But as often as we honor our ancestors by remembering their languages and invoking their ceremonies, we honor them by *not* repeating their hurtful mistakes—and by being thoughtful about how we can best serve our changing communities here and now. In some of the magical traditions I've studied, for example, there's a lot of historical and not-so-historical talk about white magic and black magic. Living as we all do under white supremacy, you can imagine which one was considered "good" and which one, "bad." I reject this as both racist and a false binary. Witchcraft—truly any magical tradition—can grow and change as it's practiced. Given the dire global situation we're in now—all of us again under financial, legislative, and psychic attack by desperate patriarchs—I propose we all provisionally initiate ourselves and get moving with some witchcraft.

Kelly Cree and Jessica Mullen, who write the *Monthly Manifestation Manual* for the School of Life Design, sum up one basic magical process this way:

1. Focus on your desire.

2. Practice feeling as if your desire is already your reality.

3. Engage physical props (for example, light a candle).

4. Give no fucks about the outcome.

So, we're looking for focus, a feeling of intention rather than want, symbolic language, and a relaxed attitude of letting go of our attachment to the results.

It's a good idea to end our magical requests with "or whatever is best for all beings in all realms" or "if it's for the greater good." That way we've got an inoculation against our own ignorance or righteousness. We want what's best for the most vulnerable, whether or not our specific visions hold the answers.

I've written ten books before this one, and every book is its own kind of spell.

When *this* book first showed up as an image in my imagination—where all things begin—I saw it coming together like one of those old synagogue or church recipe collections where you get instructions for making Madge's Meatloaf and Bubbie Eddy's Mandel Bread, mimeographed and bound with a thick, plastic spiral. Only *this* ladies' auxiliary cookbook is about toppling the patriarchy before we make dinner—because it's gone on too long.

It truly has.

Its time has come.

Patriarchy—the age-old system that enforces a gender binary and creates brutal hierarchies among men while universally privileging the masculine over the feminine—hurts all of us. It forces us to act as if men don't need relationships, women don't need selves, and trans and nonbinary people have no right to exist at all. We reject that system.

We're over the endless destruction that seems to be the only skill of toxic hypermasculinity. We're over unrepentant rapists being handed judicial positions where they're allowed to have authority over women's bodies. No good has come of patriarchy, and if those entitled white men aren't willing to step away from positions of power, we will use every tool in our arsenal—from the everyday to the otherworldly—to undermine them and ultimately remove them.

It seems to me that the orthodox religions always know more about the devil than I do and can describe him in more detail, and if I hadn't a nice type of mind I'd begin to wonder what company they keep when the moon rides high in the sky and good witches are doing simple little incantations and asking for spiritual guidance.

Magic doesn't require that we convert to a different religion or adopt any religion at all. Witches are pagan, Christian, Jewish, Muslim, Buddhist, Hindu, Sufi, agnostic, atheist, and anything else they happen to be. Witchcraft comes to us from every language that has ever existed, so some of us spell magic with a *c* and some of us spell magick with a *ck* and we don't need to jump to assimilate our differences. If there's anything in these pages you don't care to try, feel free to skip it. *Bubbie Eddy doesn't care.*

But consider the possibility that it's the patriarchy itself that put the fear of witchcraft in us.

So let's divest from belief in the devil.

Keep making the connections.

Experiment.

Question dominating language.

Trust your own authority.

Listen to people more marginalized than yourself.

Adapt.

Feel free to use the spells in this book in any order you like. The A–Z progression works beautifully. Or you can start by spelling out your own name. If I were taking that approach, I'd begin with:

Ancestors
Reclaiming Power
Infinite Intelligence
Essential Oils
Lunar Love

Or maybe you'll get out your ouija board with its ABCs and let spirit point your way.

You can try the spells by yourself, with a buddy, or in a small group. Thirteen is a traditional maximum size for a coven. But if you can't think of twelve other people you can stand, fewer is totally cool.

It will magnify our power to sometimes perform hexes simultaneously, so I invite us all to coordinate with other magic-makers in hexing the patriarchy at scheduled times. Working alone or with a group at other times is effective and wonderful, too, as each spell will echo and amplify the others through time and space.

You don't have to wear a black hat or dress up in a gauzy outfit or dance naked in the forest. It's better to be yourself. Dress how you dress. You don't even have to believe anything. Magic is simply a way of cultivating personal power and uncovering our inherent divinity.

You'll notice that some of the spells in this collection are designed to very actively hex those who are abusing their power—we'll learn to bind them with the letter *B* and to send psychic servitors to do our bidding in the courts and Congress with the letter *S*. Other spells focus on taking care of what we love, and on preserving and restoring our own energy. We'll protect the moon, for example, with the letter *L*'s "lunar love" and exchange energy with trees with the letter *T*.

Individually and cumulatively, the spells here are intended to destroy the patriarchy and invite us all to find strength in our own roots and experiences rather than falling for the old "you need the patriarchy to survive" line.

Because we don't.

We don't need it.

It's not serving our communities.

So we're pulling the plug.

We're working daily in the steady development of personal power and community power in the pursuit of a world beyond this white supremacist, capitalist war machine that depends on misogyny as its helix foundation.

And we control the power sources.

So when we say we're pulling the plug,

Well,

It's

Done.

THE HEX TALK

The word *hex* comes to us from the same mother word as *hag*—Hagazussa, the wild sorceress in Nordic mythology who straddles the fence between the mortal world and the spirit world.

Before the Inquisition, the word *hex* meant a slut, or a comedian, or a woman who flew through the sky at night. *Doesn't it make you happy that those three pastimes were synonymous?*

Slut.
Comedian.
Witch.

After the inquisition, *hex* came to mean *witch*. As in, a person who practiced magic. As in, *Hey, Hex, wanna grab lunch and put a pox on your bully neighbors?*

Heks still means *witch* in Dutch, Norwegian, and Polish.

In Pennsylvanian German, *hexe* became a verb meaning "to *practice* witchcraft."

And a little over a hundred years ago, its English meaning morphed closer to current usage, so that it now suggests casting a spell. While some people only use the word *hex* when talking about negative spells, we're going to use the word more neutrally and positively here. Like, *Hey, Hex, come help if you can—We're pulling the plug on this bullshit right here.*

See *hag.*

What would it look like "to hag the patriarchy"?

Hags get a bad rap.

But I like hags.

I aspire to be a most powerful hag.

Hagazussa says: *Don't use hexes to harm anyone unless you'd sign off on the same punishment for your own son—or cat—should he be discovered to be exploiting others in the same way.*

Consider the implications. I'm not here to preach.
It's your birthright as a witch to hex. Just sayin'.
My teacher told me that to hex someone is to bind them
to you forever. I have not found that to be so. And if
I am forever bound to Brock Turner as the witch
who hexed him, so be it. I am a strong witch, and
he's the one who is watching his back.

—MELANIE HEXEN, Iowan grandmother and midwife

Many traditions teach us that whatever we put out there comes back at us threefold. So don't put anything out there you wouldn't feel comfortable having triple-boomeranged back in your face.

Think about that.

On the other hand, this is true: oppressed people have survived by sometimes hexing their tormentors.

Easy rule: don't do anything unnecessarily dickish.

Instead, entertain possibility.

Strengthen who and what you love.

Divest from patriarchy.

Invest in sexual liberation.

Divest from the binary gender system.

Invest in respect.

Divest from systemic and individual oppression.

Invest in equity.

Divest from white supremacy.

Invest in social justice.

Divest from capitalism.

Invest in community economics.

Break things when necessary.

It's OK to be you.

You can say that out loud:

> *It's OK to be me!*

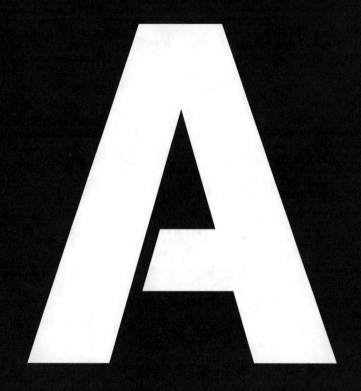

ANCESTORS

The ancestor of the letter *A* is the kabbalistic *ALEPH*, derived from a hieroglyph of an ox's head—associated with the badass horned goddess Hathor. Along with *β*, or *BET*, we get *ALEPH-BET*.

Hit Up Your Dead Relatives To Help You Smash The System

What do you know about your great-great-grandmother?

What can you guess?

All indigenous people had magical folk traditions—and all of us have ancestors who were indigenous to *somewhere*. So, if your great-great-grandmother wasn't a witch herself, she surely descended from one. In that sense, we're all the children and grandchildren of a witch they never managed to burn—or a witch who procreated first. Think about that.

One of my ancestors was hanged as a witch back in Salem. But she was already a grandmother by the time they got her. It's unlikely she was even practicing an old religion at that point, but she did own some choice real estate the patriarchs wanted.

Another distant relative of mine testified against her. Witch hunting was a highly profitable business.

The mestizo and indigenous witches of Abiquiu, near where I live now in Northern New Mexico, put up a valiant magical fight against Spanish colonization and forced Christianization. Reports described sorcerers turning themselves into cats and owls to fight the good fight, and they famously made Father Juan José Toledo so sick—with a giant moveable ball growing in his stomach!—that he had to beg a local *curandera* to save his life. The magical dissidents were tried for witchcraft in the mid-eighteenth century, long after the Salem witch trials, but the convicted witches weren't murdered.

Many of us are mash-ups of various ancestries—the children and grandchildren of so many diasporas. And the people in our families who carried the magical traditions are often those least likely to have their names show up in government documents: your illiterate grandmother, the aunt who never got her papers, the father unnamed on your birth certificate.

If you were adopted into a family you're not to related to by DNA, you have the option to claim and accept *either* the adoptive or the ancestral line—or *both*, making you double badass.

Don't ever worry if you don't know the names of your ancestors. Your ancestors all know who *you* are. And right here, right now, all of your witchy lines are calling on you to focus your power.

Like our DNA, our magical traditions are often mash-ups, too. Immigrants bring their gods, charms, and spells to new homelands. Our inheritances are mergings. Because of the history of West African enslavement, those traditions have had particularly sweeping global influence. Because of Irish enslavement, the Jewish diaspora, Romani nomadism, pogroms, and all kinds of other forced migration, we find the spiritual strategies of the oppressed all over the world, infused in every religion.

Magic thrives in temporary encampments, in kitchens and squats, in red-light districts and beauty salons, in prisons and quilting circles, on disputed borders and in low-wage workplaces of every kind. I mean, when I say "money magnetism" at an adjunct professor meeting, *everybody* starts taking notes.

Different traditions use different doors to access the unseen world, but the underlying philosophies of moral liberation are often surprisingly similar.

That said, if you work with traditions you have no family, community, or cultural connection to, it's your responsibility to educate yourself. Don't use other people's traditions to aggrandize yourself. If you're white or cis-male, prioritize listening. Stand back from leadership roles and give others space to speak and thrive.

The spells in this book are all offered freely in a spirit of sharing and experimentation to anyone willing to lay down the weapons of privilege—meaning that you're expressly invited to use them!—but if you want to dig further into traditions you're not otherwise connected to, be mindful of your role as a guest. Colonizing rituals and symbols you think are "exotic" by claiming them as your own in order to hex the patriarchy defeats the purpose and perpetuates white supremacy.

Supremacy Smashing Spell for Beginners

For the first spell of the alphabet, we're going to try something very straightforward: writing a spell against supremacy. Here's how:

Gather

An altar

Writing supplies

Candle

Incense

Begin

1. If you don't already have an altar, build one. It can be very simple, perhaps a special piece of cloth covering a table, with pictures of ancestors—meaning anyone powerful in your life who has passed on, even if they were younger than you or not related to you by blood. Include stones or trinkets or other things that are meaningful to you.

2. Write your spell by stating simply what you intend to manifest.

3. Stand in front of your altar with your spell. Focus on your intentions. Close your eyes and practice feeling as if your desire is already your reality.

4. Engage a prop or two—light a candle or some incense. You may choose to address your ancestor or ancestors directly, calling on them for power.

5. When you feel done, thank your ancestors and say good-bye for now.

Neesha Powell-Twagirumukiza has some tips for getting started with ally-ancestors. An Atlanta-based writer whose work I first started following on the online magazine and social network *Autostraddle,* Neesha comes from a long line of southern Black witches with the gift of discernment. When seeking healing, Neesha doesn't call on the church that raised them, but on the power and self-determination of their ancestors who include domestic workers, sharecroppers, and enslaved people. They invite you to hit up your own thoughtful ancestors, too—including adopted ancestors who may not be related to you but inspire you.

Which of your ancestors can you shout to for strength?

Spell Against White Supremacy

NEESHA POWELL-TWAGIRUMUKIZA

I define magic as creating desired change by performing rituals for those who guide and protect me, whether they be ancestors, African goddesses, or natural wonders.

Magic is easier for me to digest than the southern Black Baptist tradition that raised me. That tradition taught me to depend on cis-gender heterosexual men to guide my spirituality. It taught me to be ashamed of things that I find pleasurable. When I think about the Black church, I can't help but think of white slave owners pacifying enslaved Black folks who they perceived as savages with the lessons of Christianity. I often feel nostalgic about the Black church, and I honor its participation in social justice movements. However, I don't feel welcome there anymore as a genderqueer feminist since most Black churches adhere to gender roles that disempower women and LGBTQ+ people.

Alternatively, the word *magic* fills my head with images of enslaved Black people preserving their ancestral deities in the Americas by practicing Voodoo and Santería. Magic is an ancestral practice that transcends time and oceans. To me, magic means resilience and connecting to ancestors who survived the tragedy of the Middle Passage. Magic runs through my veins and feels like my birthright. It's stronger than white supremacy will ever be.

White supremacy forces us to draw our strength from anti-Blackness, heterosexism, and patriarchy. I use magic in my everyday life to combat individual and systemic oppression.

I write spells to manifest positive things in my own life and the lives of my beloveds. I write spells for the healing and liberation of my communities. The first thing I do when writing a spell is find out what's happening in the sky. Sometimes the planets are aligned just right to cast an effective spell. Major celestial events such as lunar eclipses amplify the potency of our magic.

Then, I decide who to direct my spell toward. I choose the ancestors or spirit guides who have the power to give me what I need. I'm always adding new names to this roster. Lately, I've been learning about Obatala, a West African orisha who is said to have created humans. I feel a kinship with this androgynous orisha who completely disregards gender and protects disabled people. I see myself in Obatala's image, and I feel held by them as someone living with disabilities.

Someone else I honor during spells is Nyabingi, a Rwandese-Ugandan woman warrior who fought fiercely against European colonizers in the early 1900s. My Rwandese partner introduced me to Nyabingi, who's now a possibility model for both of us.

When performing spells together, my partner and I also invoke our late grandmothers. My maternal grandmother, Carolyn, was a devout Christian, but how she lived her life was magic. Grandma was a compassionate lady whose many gifts were stifled by Jim Crow and patriarchy. She accepted everyone for who they were, grew thriving plants despite living in a small apartment, and whipped up soul food that tasted like love feels. Wherever she is, my grandma is shaking her head at the white men abusing their power and privilege. I see her face every time I stand at my personal altar, adorned with photos (including hers), trinkets from friends and family, and art made by queer and trans people of color. This is where I cast my spells.

While casting spells, I channel the strength that allowed my grandma to survive during an era when Black women were disenfranchised at every turn. The words in my spells are less important than the intention behind them. My spells are straightforward, stating exactly what I want to manifest and calling on the power of spirit to make it happen. Spell-writing is my time for reflection, meditation, and gratitude. I cherish my ritual of casting spells at my altar alone, with my partner, and with other loved ones.

What would it look like for Black, Brown, trans, and queer folks to include magic in our resistance against white supremacy? I'm hoping that we can begin reclaiming magic and redefining it for ourselves.

B

BINDING

In the Runic alphabet
Futhark, ß represents
the birch tree and
symbolizes the feminine,
growth, and renewal.

STOP GRABBY ASSHOLES BY TYING UP ALL THEIR APPENDAGES

In the last few years, a massive and global circle of witches has begun virtually meeting every waxing moon to name and bind powerful patriarchs. Their work is reversing the tides. As we join them, let's remember to protect ourselves.

A binding spell is a way to symbolically tie up a particular target, restricting his actions. But when we work with social justice, by extension we work with injustice. When we hex the patriarchy, we handle patriarchal energy. A concern when witches do spells to bind dangerous leaders or exes or

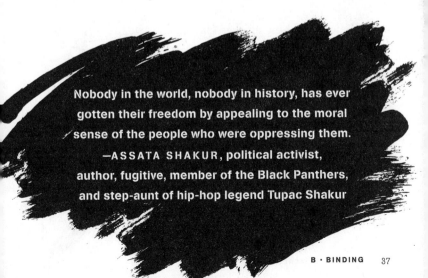

Nobody in the world, nobody in history, has ever gotten their freedom by appealing to the moral sense of the people who were oppressing them.
—ASSATA SHAKUR, political activist, author, fugitive, member of the Black Panthers, and step-aunt of hip-hop legend Tupac Shakur

ideologies is that we may inadvertently bind ourselves to that person or his mind-set. Similarly, when we invest ourselves blindly in fighting The Man, we can get stuck in his world. So, let's be careful of that.

When in doubt, prioritize self-preservation.

You can begin by using salt scrubs to wash away patriarchal bullshit. Spiritual cleansing and clearing get rid of shitty vibes that can stick to objects, places, and living things.

In all the magical traditions I've been taught, salt is used to purify, to cleanse, and to protect. (It's also used to attract money.) We throw a pinch of salt over our left shoulder, into the patriarch's eye. We don't even have to look back to see if he's standing there. We'd rather not. We've learned the art of the cold shoulder by now. We protect ourselves. We create alternatives. Here's how to do it:

1. Before anything else, go outside and sweep your doorstep.

2. Come back inside and make yourself a salt scrub, using the recipe on the next page.

Anti-Patriarchal-Bullshit Salt Scrub

Gather

1 cup sea salt or Himalayan pink salt

½ cup coconut, almond, or avocado oil

5 drops rosemary essential oil or
1 teaspoon dried rosemary

5 drops lavender essential oil or
1 teaspoon dried lavender

A few drops tea tree oil

1 teaspoon crushed, dried herbs, such as sage,
angelica root, and other local herbs traditionally
used for cleansing and protection

1 jar

Begin

1. Combine salt and oil in jar.

2. Add protective herbs.

3. Mix until the herbs are fully coated by the salt and oil.

Keep your salt scrub in the shower or next to your sink, and cleanse yourself with it whenever you work with dying ideologies.

With the trust that you're ready now, my buddy Lasara Firefox Allen, author of *Sexy Witch* and *Jailbreaking the Goddess*, offers this technique she's found effective for binding the past so as to live in and grow from the present—and into a feminist future. Feel free to adapt it to bind anything you need to bind.

Binding the Past

LASARA FIREFOX ALLEN

Binding is an act of sympathetic magick. You can bind energy or the actions of people, yourself or others.

Binding our collective history will help to keep us in the place where we have the most power: firmly in the present. Only in the present do we have the power of choice. Only in the present do we have the ability to look forward and set positive intentions. In the present, we have the ability to create new answers to old questions. Are you ready? Let's begin.

Gather

Art or writing supplies

Scissors

Yarn or thread (I use black or white, but use whatever color you think appropriate)

1 taper candle (for wax to seal the binding)

Prepare

If you have a relationship with a deity you think would be helpful in this binding—particularly one who can protect you—feel free to invoke that deity before you begin.

Begin

1. You're going to create an artifact that represents the histories and collective our-stories that need to be bound. Your artifact can be a piece of writing, a drawing or painting, a sculpture, or anything you feel moved to create. It can be very simple, such as a few words on a piece of paper, or something more time consuming to create.

2. Take the yarn or thread, long enough to tie around your artifact three times, and as you wrap it, think of the stories, emotions, and images you're binding. Imagine them becoming tied and bound, unable to affect you anymore. If it helps you to speak while you work, you can say, *I bind you, I bind you, I bind you,* as many times as feels right. If you've invoked a deity, you may also choose to invoke the name of the deity to aid the binding. For example: *In the name of .... , I bind you.*

3. Place the bound artifact on your altar or in another place of power. This artifact, this story, is a part of your history, and you can claim it. By so doing, you claim your wounds and allow yourself permission to heal. This bound artifact now represents a past that is contained and a future that is wide open for growth.

4. If you like, you may keep your bound object on your altar. It's bound after all. If it feels more cathartic to destroy it, burn it.

5. Once it's safely burnt to a fine ash (in a bowl, bucket, or cauldron), you may release the ash on a water force running away from you. This may be a stream or a river—but the kitchen sink drain will do.

BLESSED BINDING.

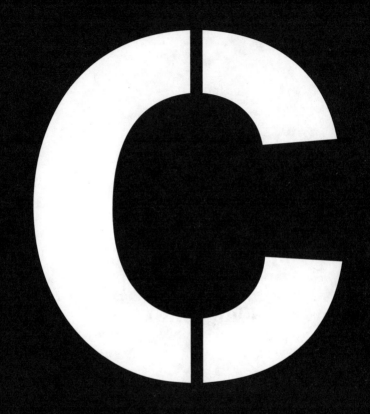

C

CONJURE

The crescent-shaped
☾ is associated
with the tarot's high
priestess. Conjure
potential into reality.

Quietly Erode Patriarchal Power With Poetry, Antlers, And Too Much Eyeliner, Bruja

---

I want you to breathe this word *conjure*.

Conjure is *con*, meaning "together," plus *jurare*, "to swear."

We're swearing together here.

We call upon our ancestors for support, we bind specific patriarchs and ideologies the way we might restrain a three-hundred-pound psychotic toddler on a rampage, and then we use Conjure to start manifesting what we *do* want in the world.

Conjure—the word, the practice—has so many excellent uses. Conjuring in the kitchen means you know how to put together a delicious meal from whatever you've got in the fridge. Conjure is DIY. Conjuring from the herb cupboard means that whatever ails us will soon be cured. Conjure comes in handy when we're poor.

I once conjured a needed job for myself by sprinkling the top of a green seven-day candle with orange and cinnamon oil, dusting it with a little gold glitter, and writing into the wax "Ariel Gore works at (name of employer)," as if it was already true, and then lit the wick. Of course, I also applied for the job—you might be surprised how many beginner witches skip this step and then come crying to Mama that their spell didn't work! So, yes, I *applied* for the job, and then, on the way to the interview when I started to get that nervous unworthy feeling, I reminded myself that in the unseen world I already *had* the position: so as long as it was best for all beings in all realms, it was a done deal.

Try this:

Conjure Utopia

Gather

1 purple seven-day candle, or a candle made with amethyst-infused wax

Lavender oil

Silver glitter

Begin

1. Sprinkle the candle with the lavender oil.

2. Dust it with the silver glitter.

3. Write into the wax your wish, such as: All people have free access to birth control.

4. As you light the candle, envision that future as if it's already true.

Of course, you can write any message you want. What do you need? What does your community need? In your mind's eye, see if you can shift that sense of need into a sense of the need already being fulfilled and cast the spell in that spirit.

Conjuring can take time; that's true. Tiffany Haddish, queen of comedy and author of *The Last Black Unicorn*, recently told *Glamour* magazine, "My thoughts from two years ago is what's happening right now. I really think my thoughts are my magic wand."

And they are!

We're here to tap that kind of manifestation—even if things take a couple of years.

Conjure is a verb, but it's a patient verb.

Conjure means to conspire.

Conjure can make things appear by magic or *as if* by magic—it's all the same to us.

If we say we've "conjured something up," we don't necessarily mean that the *only* ingredient was magic, but we're empowered by the fact that at least one of the ingredients was magic. We combine intention with other strategies to increase and secure our power.

If we say that someone is "a name to conjure with," we mean they're powerful.

I'd say the *bruja* poet MK Chavez is a name to conjure with. The author of *Mothermorphosis* and *Dear Animal,* and codirector of the Berkeley Poetry Festival, MK has a shy smile that functions as a stealthy decoy. She's an embodied belief in the power of literary confrontation to obliterate oppression. MK taught me this poem-spell to read aloud any time of the day or night. It has the power to erode the patriarchy as we conjure strength in ourselves. Try it.

Brujita Spell to Wear Down the Patriarchy

MK CHAVEZ

The ocean will assist you with the unexpected.

■

Turn three times under a dark sky,
rummage through bins at thrift stores
until you find treasures,
offer coins to a tree,
bathe in the billow of *palo santo,*
write a letter and put it in a box.

■

Speak in tongues—
deja la lengua libre.

■

Carry a blood quartz,
wrap velvet around your neck,
take a selfie, look at the *dios* and
diosa in you.

■

Have a séance for the living.

■

Pretend you have antlers,
do what the deer do.

■

Conspire.
Conspire again.

■

Scry into a bowl of clear water,
conjure the wild.

■

Put on too much eyeliner, Bruja,
and too much lipstick too.
Invoke the strength of swan.
Stay up until the dark hours of the morning,
en la madrugada, before the cock crows
imagine the patriarchy
fading in the morning's early light.

■

D

DRAGON
MYSTERIES

The letter *D* developed
from the logogram image
of an open tent door.
If you're not a meanie,
come on in.

Slay Your Inner
White Supremacist

We find dragons in almost every mythology that's ever existed. Dragons represent all the elements: they breathe fire, fly through the air, live in muddy rivers and the deep sea, and emerge from floods and chaos.

Some people think the global mythologies are so similar because dragons once existed. If you've seen alligators and crocodiles up close—or studied pterodactyl skeletons—dragons don't seem that far-fetched. At the paleontological dig sites at Ghost Ranch, or Rancho de las Brujas, in Abiquiu, New Mexico, the dinosaur fossils sure look like they might have been dragons.

Some people think that, OK, maybe the dragons never lived among us. But the legends live *in* us, bone deep, giving us our instinctual fear of snakes.

But dig this: many magical truths, traditions, and symbols are cross-cultural. When humans around the world share similar belief systems, that sometimes suggests those groups made contact. Ancient travel routes have been completely underreported because of racist historians' inability to accept that advanced ancient civilizations existed and moved about the planet long before it ever occurred to European conquerors that the world wasn't flat.

But physical contact isn't necessary.

Channeled and dreamtime spirits aren't slowed down by oceans or border walls.

The protective qualities of Arnica were discovered wherever it grew.

No one needs a missionary to teach them how to fuck.

And dragons—they have this universal tendency to show up.

Take Rhea Wolf, a nice queer mom who helps organize and facilitate the Pagan Gathering Services in the women's prison at Coffee Creek in Oregon. Rhea never cared about dragons one way or another. Then Red Dragon appeared to her in a dream, and look at them now—partners in their mission to tear down the racist patriarchy with words and witchcraft. Rhea uses the imagery and energy of the red dragon—which was also channeled by witches in the 1980s to fight AIDS—to slay racism and supremacist ideologies and heal from the trauma those systems inflict. The idea here is both to retrieve the energy the system has taken from us and then to use that energy to smash the system, *bam!*

Try the exercises as Rhea has laid them out, and then experiment and see where the red dragon takes you.

Red Dragon Spells of Liberation
from Supremacy Ideologies

Rhea Wolf

Song of the Red Dragon

Red heart ▪ Earth heart ▪ Down deep
▪ Ancient wisdom flowing

Rise up ▪ Everywhere ▪ Dreamwalk
▪ To the beautiful, beautiful future

Hexing is a form of powerful protection magic, but it's also a rigorous examination of the harm being caused by ourselves and others. To hex someone else, we have to acknowledge the ways we participate in the harming of self and others, while empowering other parts of ourselves that have fallen into the role of prey.

For over a year, I've been working a spell that involves monthly ritual, daily reflection, hexing, healing, and research. The spell has been guided by Red Dragon, a multidimensional being who can exist in simultaneous spaces and times. I first met Red Dragon about fifteen years ago in a dream. I had no prior connections to dragons, hadn't even thought about them very much. But Red Dragon lifted me up in the dream, danced with me, and told me that I was born to ride with them.

A few years later, I learned from a teacher of mine that some witches in the 1980s had been called on by Red Dragon to heal HIV-AIDS. Shortly after completing their spell work, the triple cocktail of drugs came about, effectively reversing the death sentence for those with the virus. This linked Red Dragon to the witchcraft of healing but also liberation from dominant paradigms that oppress groups of people.

One night, I asked for spiritual guidance about how I could use witchcraft to heal racism and supremacy ideologies in myself and the world. Red Dragon came back to me in dreams and told me this spell.

The Red Dragon lives in our blood, so we can always connect to them. As a blood dragon, they also live in the waters of the world, ley lines, and deep in Earth. The Red Dragon spell itself is ongoing and being created by all of us witches who are working antiracist, antidomination, antioppression magic. There are so many ways to tap into it—from prayer to doing more involved spell work, to running the Red Dragon pentacle.

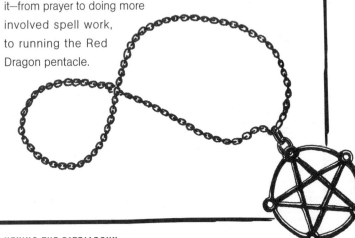

Run the Red Dragon Pentacle

To run the pentacle, stand with your arms out to the sides and your feet in a wide stance. Your body makes a five-pointed star when you do that! You're a pentacle. Now, psychically run energy through your body—just imagine energy running from each point of the pentacle, infusing your whole self with the qualities that each point holds:

1. Start at your head (that's chaos at the top of the pentacle)
2. Then run the energy down to your right foot (life)
3. Then up to the left hand (rhythm)
4. Then across the heart to the right hand (time)
5. Then down to the left foot (flow)
6. Then back up to the head (chaos)

After you do this a few times, psychically run a circle around you from your head (*chaos*), to your left hand (*rhythm*), to your left foot (*flow*), to right foot (*life*), to your right hand (*time*), and back to your head (*chaos*). Each point contains its own world.

See what you find.

Red Dragon Incantation

Find a quiet place to concentrate on your intention. Then, say this out loud:

> I call on the Red Dragon who lives in the blood to unravel and heal transgenerational wounds of racism in the DNA, to help me personally surrender attachment to the power of white privilege and supremacy, and to support the regeneration and healing of our DNA to support liberation for all of Earth's peoples.

∎

Red Dragon Healing

Each new moon, I set an intention of surrender for that specific lunar cycle. The action or qualities of my monthly surrender are informed by the zodiac, as the moon moves through the astrological signs. The new moons identify what form of white power and supremacy ideologies I must surrender each month. One a month. Start with the one that's next on the horizon—depending on when in the lunar cycle this spell finds you.

To heal all forms of hierarchical domination from misogyny to ableism requires a surrender of attachment to the following:

New moon in Aries: Surrender anger and defensiveness.

New moon in Taurus: Surrender resistance to life—resistance to change.

New moon in Gemini: Surrender dualism and intentional confusion.

New moon in Cancer: Surrender nationalism and personal security.

New moon in Leo: Surrender selfishness.

New moon in Virgo: Surrender judgment without values.

New moon in Libra: Surrender superficiality and anaesthetic responses.

New moon in Scorpio: Surrender desire for control, which is fear of death.

New moon in Sagittarius: Surrender the need for Truth with a capital T.

New moon in Capricorn: Surrender power over others.

New moon in Aquarius: Surrender ideology.

New moon in Pisces: Surrender victimization and the illusion of separation.

ESSENTIAL OILS

The most commonly used
letter in our alphabet,
E, descends from the
Egyptian hieroglyph that
pictures a little human
figure with its hands up in
prayer or party mode. Give
it up for the shutdown of
the patriarchy.

Concentrate Perfume
To Become Your Own Goddess And
Run Abusive Liars Out Of Town

The first time I moved to Santa Fe, the best deal I could find on an apartment was more of a live-work space—a storefront with a studio apartment upstairs. So I did what you do when you stumble into a storefront: I opened a witch shop.

My then two-year-old son, Maxito, loved being a wizard. With his little spray bottle of vinegar water and a wad of newspaper, he carefully cleaned the glass display cases that held our mystical supplies.

Our business took off right away, of course. We had walls of seven-day candles, shelves of essential oils, giant glass jars filled with local herbs, and a back corner that served as a comfy antiquarian library. We sold Santería, Wiccan, tarot, orisha, and Hoodoo supplies. I put together Saint Joseph kits to move real estate and blended Gammie Evelyn's Face Oil to keep everyone moisturized in the desert. Witchy and curious people came in for love spells and protection charms, employment candles and nettles.

> I learn from no one book. I study as I please. I follow a trail
> of biblio-breadcrumbs. I read the writing in the leaves.
> —PAM GROSSMAN, *What Is a Witch*

I learned fast who'd cursed whom in Santa Fe, who'd lost and found romance, who was on the run from the law, who needed fast cash, and who had cash to give.

I learned some of the thousand and one different ways that magic is practiced, both within and without formal religion, in one Western American town. And I had the pleasure of hand-selling essential oils blended by one of my godmothers, Vajra Conjure Wright.

People have been anointing themselves and their magical tools with oil pretty much forever—we see references to and evidence of anointing in early Buddhist and Hindu traditions, in indigenous Australia, in the Middle East, in North Africa, and in Greek mythology. The goal: to make ourselves and whatever we rub with oil divine.

In the 1100s, Ibn al-Baitar, an Andalusian pharmacist and chemist, upped the game when he invented *essential* oils—basically the super-concentrated energies of various plants. So now instead of just anointing every wand or candle with whatever generic fat or oil we have around, we could get really specific. For example, we might dress a candle with rose oil to manifest love. I myself anoint daily with a white sandalwood musk, honey-suckle, and bergamot blend called De Faya that Vajra blends to give me a gutsy glamour and an almost military authority as I go about my business undermining hurtful power structures.

Vajra started making her own perfumes and ritual oils when she was a young teenager training to become a classical guitarist. Now a practicing witch in Portland, Oregon, her path included a goth rock transformation and ultimately ordination as a priest of the orisha Elegua in the Santería tradition.

On Friday, July 13, 2007, Vajra shaved off her eyebrows, drew new ones on, and officially hung out her shingle for her shop, Conjure Oils: Fine Fragrances Both Sacred and Profane.

However we use essential oils—by anointing ourselves, candles, or other magical tools—the effect turbo-powers our spells and intentions. Vajra's **Repelling Oil**, for example, made with eucalyptus and devil's shoestrings, can be used to drive away harassers. Her **Smackdown Oil**, made with deer's tongue, red pepper, poppy seeds, and vandal root, can be used to annihilate anyone who messes with Maxine Waters. **Strength Oil**, on the other hand, made with peony and High John the Conqueror root, increases our own and our allies' stamina.

I asked Vajra to share her most effective secret blends to hex The Man and send him packing.

It Takes 10,000 Roses
to Fill a Teaspoon

VAJRA CONJURE WRIGHT

Essential oils are ethereal oils, meaning they're the essence—or the soul—of the plant. It's always important to respect essential oils and protect yourself when producing a blend. Never let pets or children be exposed to essential oils. Never eat them. They are potent—it takes ten thousand roses to fill a teaspoon.

There are several kinds of magickal oil blends. I am familiar with two—Hoodoo and Western magickal traditions. Hoodoo is African American folk magick with an admixture of Native American herbalism as well as Jewish occultism and magick. In Hoodoo, we can access supernatural forces through candle and oil magick.

In the Western tradition, we see many oils named after deities, elements, planets, and astrological signs. They are used by anointing a candle or an amulet.

There are two oils you can make to smash the patriarchy. The first is a formula that I created for personal power. We need to empower ourselves daily, so every day when you get up apply the oil to your heart, third eye, and the crown of your head, saying a small prayer to your goddess (you can be your own goddess if you wish.) The second formula is a traditional Hoodoo mixture using some nasty stuff.

Here are the recipes:

Personal Power Oil

Gather

10–20 drops bergamot essential oil

5–10 drops jasmine oil (fragrance oil is fine
if you can't obtain true jasmine)

5–10 drops frankincense oil

10–15 drops sandalwood or cedar wood oil

5–10 drops rose otto essential oil
(fragrance oil is fine if you can't get true rose)

A tiny piece of dragon's blood and/or
an open safety pin*

1 drop of your own blood
(prick any finger with a rose thorn or a lancet)

Fractionated coconut (often called MCT),
jojoba, or sunflower oil

1 drop vitamin E oil (if using sunflower oil
to keep it from going rancid)

1 one-ounce bottle

* Dragon's blood is a bright red resin derived from a number of
different plants available at most spiritual supply stores. If you
don't have dragon's blood, place the open safety pin in the
bottle instead.

Begin

In the bottle, combine the essential oils, resin or
open safety pin, and blood. Fill the rest of the bottle
with the coconut, jojoba, or sunflower oil.

Hot Foot Oil

When

Start this on the new moon and let it sit
until the next new moon.

Gather

A small handful of dried red peppers

2 tablespoons black peppercorns

2 tablespoons kosher salt

1 tablespoon powdered sulphur

Mineral oil

1 eight-ounce mason jar or
other small glass container

Begin

Combine all the ingredients, except the
mineral oil, in the jar. Fill the jar with
mineral oil and shake it every so
often over the month.

Always wash your hands after using
Hot Foot Oil. There are lots of uses
for Hot Foot Oil. Look them up.
We use Hot Foot to send our enemies
packing—and running. Try the following
retaliation spell with your first batch
of homemade Hot Foot Oil.

Retaliation Spell

When

Best done a couple days before the new moon.

Gather

Photograph of the patriarch you're after

1 black candle

Hot Foot Oil

Pins

Begin

1. Slather the candle with the oil. Rub it away from you, going from the base of the candle to the tip. As you do so, imagine you're ridding yourself of anything negative you want out of your life, imagine it coming out of you and into the candle. Let your anger, pain, stress, depression, and anxiety fill the candle: you'll be sending it to your target.

2. Affix the photo with pins to the candle, and pray to the darkest goddesses you can think of (remember, you can be your own goddess) to remove your tormentor.

3. Light the candle and sit there feeling the emotions that sit like a lava stone in the pit of your stomach and let them burn out.

For those people who fear retaliation spells, or who believe in karma or the threefold law, you can do this spell, just don't direct it at anyone in particular. Use it to target depression, anxiety, and shame.

FIGHT SONG

The letter *F* originates with the Egyptian symbol for a club. So *F* has always known how to fight. It didn't become a bad grade until 1898 when professors at Mount Holyoke College worried that if we'd completely blown it in one of their classes, we might also be too thick to realize *E* didn't stand for excellent. So they went with *F* to more clearly signal our total fail. To them we say, *FU*.

Use Anthems To Psych Yourself Up For Confrontations With The Man

One of the ways the patriarchy undermines us is by making us feel like shit for everything from our waistlines to our leadership styles. By bombarding us with messages of unworthiness, these trolls hope to effectively disarm us so we'll stay home shame-spiraling instead of hitting the streets and kicking their asses. To counter this, a witch needs an anthem.

Considering what we're up against, we need a whole playlist of anthems.

I conducted a witch survey of confidence-raising theme songs and turned up the usual suspects like "Eye of the Tiger" and "We Are the Champions," but I got a few excellently unexpected submissions, too, and after testing them all in the hex kitchen, found particular luck with this magical playlist for binge listening. The songs come from all genres and eras, allowing us to gather strength from twenty-six different corners of time and space. The songs work together progressively and supernaturally to become more than the sum of their parts:

SUGGESTED ANTHEMS

Nina Hagen, "Born in Xixax"
Alice Bag, "Shame Game"
Lesley Gore, "You Don't Own Me"
Poison Girls, "Take the Toys"
M.I.A., "Paper Planes"
Kimya Dawson, "Loose Lips"
Princess Nokia, "Brujas"
Destiny's Child, "Bootylicious"
Patti Smith, "Gloria," "Because the Night" (Listen to
    "Gloria" first to get centered, then "Because the
    Night" to get infected with invincibility.)
Josephine Baker, "I'm Feelin' Like a Million"
Lily Allen, "Fuck You"
T.I., "Bring 'Em Out"
Bjork, "Declare Independence"
Rocky Rivera, "Pussy Kills"
The Coup, "The Guillotine"
Santigold, "Disparate Youth"
Kamala and the Karnivores, "Tiny Steps"
Instant Girl, "Euphemized"
L7, "Shitlist"
Dolly Parton, "9 to 5"
Earth, Wind & Fire, "Boogie Wonderland"
Rihanna, "Hard"

Nina Simone, "Ain't Got No (I Got Life)"
Kesha, "Praying"
Pussy Riot, "Make America Great Again"

We can use these confidence-affirming anthems as everyday inoculations against the overall psychic attack that is the patriarchy, or we can use our playlists in a more focused way.

I asked Thursday Simpson, the queen of costuming confidence, to walk us through the use of a fight song when we need focus—and ultimate victory.

I met Thursday on a spring evening in Iowa City when she showed up to a "Fuck Shame" workshop I was facilitating with local witch Shell Feijo. Thursday wore purple velour pants, and the swish of her hips said "fuck that" to anyone who offended

her twice. A multimedia artist and cofounding editor of *OUT/CAST*, a journal for the queer and midwestern, she also composes soundtracks for her writing to highlight her overall Goth Joan Crawford aesthetic. For lack of a cooler deity, she worships a concept of her own invention she calls Feline Satan.

I think we've all met that feline.

Follow her directions when you need to meet with your boss and tell him he needs to take that reference to your "pretty smile" off your performance review.

Iron Maiden for Necessary Confrontations Ritual

THURSDAY SIMPSON

This is a spell and ritual designed to be used before confrontations where you'll be arguing for or fighting for something. Anything from meeting with a caseworker, convincing a doctor or parole officer that something is or isn't necessary, going to a store to return a faulty item for cash, or what-have-you.

One of the patriarchy's most frustrating weapons is delay—lines, late appointments. The Man is trying to create an atmosphere in which you'll lose your cool and then can be dismissed as hysterical. Don't take the bait. Instead, do this:

Begin

1. Before you leave home for your confrontation, select a song or a playlist of songs that inspires focus, strength, calmness, and clarity. It can be one song, five songs, or fifty. Intentionally choose these songs that make you feel strong, rooted, motivated, and connected to your full self, to your friends and sisters, past and present. Choose songs that ease tension and remind you what you're fighting for, that make you feel light and free. Instrumentals are good if vocals distract you.

2. When you're in transit to the site of your confrontation, listen to your playlist and take deep, intentional breaths. Let the music remind you of your strength, and let your breaths keep you calm and focused.

3. After your conflict, intentionally drink a glass of water and continue taking deep breaths.

I keep a playlist on my phone with "Hallowed Be Thy Name" by Iron Maiden and a version of "Bloody Tears" from the Castlevania video games. Last summer, my Medicaid application was rejected. I'd already made several trips to the Department of Health and Human Services, bringing my caseworker all the documents he asked for: information on prior insurance or lack thereof, statements that proved I didn't have an income above $20,000 a year. I called the local office and made an appointment to reopen my case. I listened to both songs on repeat for the twenty-minute drive. I ended up needing to wait for an hour and a half in a room where cell phones weren't allowed, so I kept listening to the songs in my head, breathing in their melodies and breathing out their strength.

When I finally saw a new caseworker and she reopened my case, she discovered that my original caseworker hadn't logged a single document I'd given him and my original application was essentially blank when he submitted it for consideration. I had to travel back home, get all my documents, and give them to this new caseworker all over again so she could resubmit my application—the entire time, repeating "Hallowed Be Thy Name" and "Bloody Tears" on my car stereo, repeating the songs in my head in their office to stay focused.

If you get scared, return to your deep, intentional breaths. Don't be mad at yourself for being scared. The patriarchy is scary. Return to your breathing. Your sisters from before are with you, and you are with your sisters who will come later.

Regardless of the outcome, as you leave the site of your confrontation, continue taking deep, intentional breaths. If you choose to, create a new playlist of songs that encourage a sense of triumph, moving forward, solace, and completion.

GROWL

G comes to us from
Hebrew *GIMEL*, a letter of
constant transformation.
It represents the throat
and all that comes from its
hollow depths. *GRRR*.

Start Your Own Resistance Band And Sing "Good-Bye, MFers"

Music is a language of both magic and resistance. There's a reason certain kinds of music are banned at particular moments in history. There were reasons enslaved Africans weren't allowed to have drums in the United States—except in New Orleans. And reason followed that American music was born in New Orleans.

Music historian Michael Ventura connects the dots this way: "American music starts here. At least, American music as we've known it. Within ten years of Marie Laveau's death the brass bands of New Orleans would be playing sounds no one had ever heard before. How important was Voodoo, the African metaphysical system, to that time and place?"

In a word, *super* important. All the musicians who were first playing jazz in the 1880s and 1890s in New Orleans had probably been a part of the Voodoo celebrations that were held publicly until at least 1875. Most of them would have been old enough to remember Marie Laveau's dances at Congo Square when they were kids.

In the red-light district, Voodoo was considered "the true religion." Storyville madams had a reciprocal agreement not to use the services of Voodoo practitioners against each other and instead to focus their energy on tripping up abusive men and Confederate fools.

The favorite Voodoo queen of the madams in those days was Eulalie Echo. They constantly requested her services for hexes and cures. Her real name was Laura Hunter, and she raised Jelly Roll Morton—she was his *madrina,* or godmother.

So the mothers and godmothers of American music were conjurers.

Keep connecting the dots.

Keep making new music.

I asked Michelle Cruz Gonzales—Spitboy drummer, Kamala and the Karnivores guitarist, and author of *The Spitboy Rule: Tales of a Xicana in a Female Punk Band*—how she thinks we're going to finish the job against the patriarchy that our madrinas started. She offered the Grrr Hex, aka "Good-bye MFer."

Use it when you're ready to leave an abusive relationship or work scene, or to take back the power the patriarchy has robbed from you.

Grrr Hex

MICHELLE CRUZ GONZALES

Start a band

She, her, they, them

The fiercest you know

■

The one who hates bras, the one who stopped bleaching
her hair or worrying about whiskers on the chin, the one
who wears whatever they want—leggings as pants,
a house dress and naughty knee socks, an old slip.

■

You need the ones with crow's feet, stretch marks, kids in
college, husbands who survived cancer, mothers in
assisted-living facilities, the ones whose terrible fathers are
long dead, the ones who don't give such a fuck anymore, the
one whose laugh shrivels testicles, the hot and the flashy.

■

A band gives you a reason to gather

A reason to leave work early

A cover for your coven

A reason to wield sticks or an axe

■

If someone can't play

Be patient

Teach them, teach each other

Or just sing, bang a tambourine

■

Growl

Snarl

Gnash your teeth

Howl

Bear down

Thunder

■

You were born
of growls
of snarling, gnashing teeth
of cord and tissue
a yowling womb

■

A place of desire, intrigue

A feared, abject place

A place of laws, and lies, and all the
misogyny in the world

■

Good-bye, Motherfucker.
Say this, sing it over and over
Good-bye, Motherfucker!

■

HERBALISM

The letter *H* corresponds with the kabbalistic *CHETH* and takes its shape from a hieroglyph for "courtyard." As in, "I think you need an herb garden in your courtyard, Hex."

Empower Yourself With Plant Magic When Heartless Doctors Tell You "It's All In Your Head, Sweetie"

Historically, witches were herbalists, healers, counselors, and midwives. We tended to the health of our communities. And we often sourced our basic medicine from our own gardens.

You can start your witchy courtyard garden small—even just on a windowsill. Grow a few common herbs for protection and conjuring.

Rosemary, sage, and lavender like to grow where I live.

Find out which traditional herbs like to grow where you live.

When we use plants we grow ourselves or plants a friend or teacher grows, we bring that much more personal and community power to our spells and health tonics. We don't need to grow everything ourselves if that just adds to an impossible to-do list, but we can begin to think about our relationship with the land around us and begin to engage in more conscious land stewardship. We don't need witchy supplies that are mined from

Always throw spilled salt over your left shoulder.
Keep rosemary by your garden gate. Add pepper
to your mashed potatoes. Plant roses and lavender,
for luck. Fall in love whenever you can.

—ALICE HOFFMAN, *Practical Magic*

the earth or overharvested or flown and trucked in from far-off places. If we can stay super present with our gardening and other everyday magical meditations, we begin to notice that, little by little, everything we do becomes part of our spiritual practice—and then living a happy and ethical life comes more and more naturally. And as everything we do becomes conscious and focused, we become less willing to be complicit in exploitation of any kind.

When I need an anxiety-soothing remedy or a pain tincture, I call my local radical herbalist Alanna Whitney. She puts on her polka-dot bike helmet and red lipstick and delivers. The queer femme mama and head potion maker at Mettle and Loam Apothecary, Alanna advocates using public health models for integrative care. She traces plant magic through the time line of humanity and reminds us that we, like the herbs in our gardens, are of this Earth. Our connection comes naturally. (It's the disconnect that's artificial.) To hex what ails us, she prescribes heart aromatics.

Fab fact about hearts and herbalism: historians trace the classic heart shape to the seeds of the ancient silphium plant that grew in Northern Africa, not far from the Greek colony of Cyrene.

What was so special about silphium? It was basically a giant fennel plant—and women used its seeds for birth control. So the heart is a symbolic ode to reproductive freedom. *I (heart) you* means *I know my herbalism and let's not procreate against my will.*

Aromatics for the Heart

ALANNA WHITNEY

Herbal medicine—plant magic—is our birthright. Our connection to Earth is in our bones and blood.

A hundred years ago, knowledge of plant medicine was passed down matriarchal lines. Women and femmes knew how to use the plants that grew around them for healing: we learned from mothers and grandmothers and aunties how to work with a fever, and how to make medicine for scrapes and bumps and aches and pains and headaches and everything in between.

Part of how patriarchy steals our power is by severing our relationships and uprooting and upheaving connection to place, to self, to foremothers, to community, and to the world of plant medicine. We don't need to step away from regular ol' doctor medicine, but herbal medicine offers a conduit for reconnecting to our own healing, our bodies, and the places we make home.

What better hex than to unravel the tools of the oppressor?

Reclaiming connection is part of the special magic of plant medicine. As we take plants into ourselves, our physiology literally begins a rewiring process that helps our bodies remember groundedness. That's how I, a wee herbalist, hex patriarchal mores. What if everyone who walked Earth felt their feet and remembered what it is to be in communion with the natural world, which is to remember their truest and oldest power?

Start with Aromatics: Contemporary research confirms what plant people have always known—that smelly things can shift our brains and bodies to a place of calm groundedness and receptivity. Aromatics are a powerful tool of reconnection and especially helpful for those who've been wounded by the trauma wrought by patriarchy.

Burn Things: Burnables have been used to mark ceremony, transition, birth, death, and all moments sacred in almost every traditional culture. Burning plants like garden sage, rosemary, lavender, juniper, cedar, and many tree resins can be a powerful way to shift consciousness toward grounded calm.

Eat More Spices: All kitchen spices are aromatic. Oregano, basil, thyme, rosemary, cumin, coriander, garlic, and ginger not only flavor our food but actually shift our nervous system physiology and improve digestion.

Drink Aromatics: Most popular herbal teas are also aromatic: peppermint, ginger, chamomile, fennel, and rose. When you make a cup of tea and find yourself wanting to breathe it in while you're sipping, that's because of the volatile oils that comprise these aromatic herbs. Lots of standby favorites are available at any grocery store, but if you want to up your game, make your own. Here are a couple of my favorite recipes:

Heart-Centering Tea

Gather

2 parts hawthorn berries
(you can also use leaves or flowers)

1 part basil (regular kitchen basil
or holy basil, also known as tulsi)

1 part rose

■

Calm Heart Tea

Gather

Equal parts: linden, chamomile, and lemon balm

Begin

1. To make a basic herbal infusion, measure out one to three tablespoons (or a small handful) of dried herbs per cup.

2. Pour freshly boiled water over the mixture, and allow to infuse for at least fifteen minutes, or for a stronger brew, an hour or more. Strain and drink.

3. To make a larger and stronger batch, you can use a good-sized handful (or an ounce by weight) in a quart jar and allow to infuse overnight. Strain in the morning and refrigerate. An herbal tea will usually keep well in the fridge for three to five days.

I

INFINITE
INTELLIGENCE

Raise your
hand in a fist
for revolution,
and you've got
YOD,
the original
letter *I*.

Resurrect The Lost Religion Of The Suffragettes And The Abolitionists To Destroy Rape Culture

For one lovely week last May, I was invited to indulge in an artists' residency at The Future, an "Aquarian lab" and magic shop in the Witch District in Minneapolis.

Just my kind of adventure! I packed my bag and climbed on a plane.

Once I'd moved into my little studio space in the back of the magic shop, a friendly ghost began waking me up every morning at a reasonable hour to get to work. When I mentioned this magical alarm clock to Lacey Prpić Hedtke, the spiritual medium who ran the place, she told me that it might be Prince's ghost. His costumes had been made in this space back in the 1980s, and when he took off for the afterlife, Lacey put the spirit welcome mat out for him.

This pleased me greatly. Yes, I thought, Prince was here, waking me up in The Future to create magical art and hex the patriarchy.

Working in this witch shop, I felt a gust of déjà vu. It had been years since I lived in my own witch shop and I'd missed the air of it.

Lacey noticed my enamored gaze. "You're welcome to poke around," she said.

Everything smelled like rose and bergamot.

The Santa Fe witch shop I'd owned and lived in a decade earlier leaned toward the Wiccan, Santería, Mexican folk magic, and southwestern herbalism practiced in New Mexico. But here in Minneapolis, crystals and tinctures rubbed elbows with American Spiritualist texts. I found a copy of Annie Murphy's graphic biography of the spiritualist Achsa W. Sprague, *I Still Live*—along with historical texts on séances, mediumship, ectoplasm, automatic writing, and spirit photography.

When I turned around fast, I felt sure I saw my grandmother's grandmother, Ms. Esmeralda Moore, sitting at the ouija board.

Spiritualism, best known as the American-born tradition of nineteenth-century feminists and antislavery activists like Victoria Woodhull and Sojourner Truth, is still an active and living religion.

In my travels and migrations around the United States, following a trail of magical bread crumbs, I was beginning to see the regional patterns: everywhere, we have indigenous people's magic. We find more Voodoo and Hoodoo in the South—carried from Africa and the Caribbean. We feel the working brujería in the West and Southwest, areas that were part of Mexico until early 1848. We can trace Wicca and English magic as well as northern mystery traditions along the northern states

The spirits are coming back to tear your damned system of sexual slavery into tatters and consign its blackened remnants to the depth of everlasting hell.

—VICTORIA WOODHULL,
activist, trance medium, free love advocate,
stockbroker, and 1872 US presidential candidate

and down the West Coast, where northern European folks settled and the Reclaiming tradition eventually bloomed. In the Midwest and Northeast, we naturally see more Spiritualist influences.

Modern Spiritualism has roots in the Western explorations of trance states, clairvoyance, and direct contact with ghosts, but it took off as a formal tradition on the witch's New Year's Eve—March 31—in upstate New York in 1848. Neptune, the planet of the unseen, had only recently been discovered by astronomers. And while the United States land-grabbed the West from Mexico, Europe had its "Year of Revolutions," Karl Marx came out with his *Communist Manifesto*, and Marie Laveau kept busy using her professional Voodoo proceeds to purchase freedom for enslaved people in New Orleans, something strange was going on in a little cottage in Hydesville, New York.

The house had been haunted by mysterious rapping sounds for some five years, but on this night Kate and Maggie Fox, the young daughters of a psychic and a blacksmith, began to communicate with the ghostly "spirit raps." Some said the girls were pranksters, but many saw them as true delegates of the spirit world. Either way, the Hydesville Rappings would inspire a vast and radical female-dominated religious movement across the United States and England.

As Annie Murphy tells it, "Women all over began to lend their voices to spirit agency. What's more, they began to make these messages public. Women started appearing onstage while in trance to deliver spirit messages to the masses. When the spirits spoke, people listened. And the spirits had a lot to say. They called for no less than the eradication of all injustice. The abolition of slavery. Radical prison reform. Equal rights for women and an end to institutionalized marital rape and abuse."

Many mediums were the survivors of childhood illness, an experience that seemed to bring them closer to the spirit realm. Kitchen-table séances became all the rage as the northern abolitionist and free-love movements made solid contact with their spirit guides.

Some Spiritualist were Christians, but many weren't—and aren't today. They just believe in ghosts, in living people's capacity to communicate with ghosts, and in Infinite Intelligence—or the basic creative energy of the universe.

I mean, didn't *you* talk to spirits when you were a kid?

Lacey had been seeing thunderbirds and communicating with the other side since forever when, in 2000, she discovered the religion of Spiritualism and trained to be a medium. She learned the laying-on-of-hands spiritual healing that my great-grandmother's Aunt Eva practiced and authored *We Believe in Infinite Intelligence: A 21st Century Guide to Spiritualism*. I asked her to give us some instructions for meeting our own radical spirit guides—even if we haven't talked to them since we were kids.

A Spell for Infinite Intelligence

LACEY PRPIĆ HEDTKE

Want to connect with the spirit world or your spirit guides? It's really as simple as making time for those conversations and relationships. Infinite Intelligence is energy, God, the Goddess, love, creative force.

Begin with the intention of communicating with spirit. Turn off your phone, go to the park, do whatever you need to do to carve out a little uninterrupted quiet time. If you're wanting to call in a certain person's energy that is in spirit, bring a belonging of theirs or a photo of them or anything that will help you connect. If you'd rather get in touch with spirit guides or other spirit energy, just be open and willing to consider the possibility of connecting with spirit.

Begin

1. Sit down with your eyes closed and ground your feet.

2. Say out loud, *Only the highest and best energy is welcome here.*

3. Imagine yourself putting on a cape or wrapping a blanket around yourself or drawing a curtain—whatever will help you feel like you've built a protective layer between your energy and everything else swirling around out there. If it helps you get in the zone, light a candle, hold a crystal, sprinkle a li'l salt around.

4. Sit quietly and rub your hands together—imagine building energy up, like a spark between your hands.

5. Ask the spirits to come talk to you. You can talk out loud or just in your head—if you'd like to talk to a specific person, say their name. If you can, speak in the language that will resonate with them. Sing a song they were connected to. Basically, roll out the red carpet and ask them to join you. If you're connecting with a spirit guide, imagine walking down a hallway and opening a door. Who is behind it? What details can you see, hear, smell, sense? You might hear a noise, or an image or thought or phrase might pop into your head. Write it down or say it out loud.

6. Take note of what you're experiencing. Ask questions or just watch what comes to you.

7. Hang out here as long as you want. When you're ready to stop, say good-bye and do something that helps you visualize that you're disconnecting from the spirit world, like when you put on your protective cape earlier.

8. Thank the spirits and guides that came to you.

Whenever you need help or guidance, ask and your guides will be there. Be open to how that might manifest or how Infinite Intelligence might interpret that. The more you talk with spirit, the more you invite Infinite Intelligence energy into your life, the easier the conversations will become.

Remember that women took Spiritualism and ran with it—they were operating their own churches, reclaiming their place as healers and spiritual leaders. There are generations of badass, magical, loving healers, mediums, witches, and queers behind you and with you who are only getting stronger and wiser in the spirit world, and you can call on them when you're doubting yourself, feeling burnt out, or otherwise need their support. This shared energy that we're building up will get us through and will fuel the revolution.

JUSTICE JARS

One of the last letters
introduced to our alphabet,
J's tail was originally just
a little fabulous flourish
on the letter *I*. Then a
Renaissance Italian writer
of tragedies—who actually
petitioned to have quite a
few letters you've never
heard of introduced
into the alphabet—
hit pay dirt with this one,
giving jalopy, jinx, joy,
and justice something
fancy to spring from.

Bottle Up Your Rage To Quietly Influence Judicial Matters

―――――――

The first kind of justice magic I ever learned was also sweetening magic—a honey jar spell to sweeten a judge to my point of view. I've used it to sweeten judges to my own position and to support other women in custody and immigration hearings. Here's how to work it:

Honey Jar Spell

Gather

1 small jar of honey or syrup

1 small piece of paper

Court Case Powder*

1 small orange or brown candle

Court Case Oil**

  * Court Case Powder is available at most spiritual supply stores, or you can make your own by mixing a little crushed High John the Conqueror root with cinnamon.

** Court Case Oil is available at most spiritual supply stores, or you can make your own by adding a few drops of cinnamon oil and a few drops of calendula oil to a carrier oil like almond or jojoba and then adding a piece of devil's shoestring and a piece of High John the Conqueror root.

Begin

1. Take a small piece of paper and write the name of the judge or whoever you need to sweeten three times, like a list:

   Name

   Name

   Name

2. Turn your piece of paper ninety degrees sideways and write your own name—or the name of the person you're supporting—three times across, so that the woman's name crosses the judge's names, kind of like a tic-tac-toe grid.

3. Write your specific wish in a circle around the names—write this as one continuous circle of script, without spaces between the words. Don't even lift your pen to dot your i's or cross your t's. Your specific wish here can be very simple, such as

   Help me Help my kids Help me
   Help my kids Help me Help my kids

   OR

   Reunite Gloria with her son Reunite Gloria
   with her son Reunite Gloria with her son

   It's OK if you have to do a few drafts of this paper.

4. Once you've got it right, sprinkle a little Court Case Powder on your paper if you have it.

5. Fold the paper toward yourself—you're bringing the sweetness toward yourself and your perspective.

6. Open your jar of honey and have a spoonful. As you savor it, say, "As this honey is sweet to me, so

   Judge .... will be sweet to

   .... and favor ...."

7. Press your paper into your honey and close the jar tight.

8. Now rub the candle with the oil. Melt the candle to the top of the honey jar lid with hot wax and let the candle burn all the way down.

9. As you watch the flame, picture yourself or the person you're supporting calm, self-preserving, factual, and persuasive.

Do this candle-burning step every Monday, Wednesday, and Friday for as long as the case goes on, and say, whenever you think of it: *As this honey is sweet to me, so will Judge _____ be sweet to _____ and favor _____ .*

If you're unable to gather the physical props called for in this or any other spell, vivid visualization will work just fine. Keeping picturing yourself—or the person you're supporting— calm, self-preserving, factual, and incredibly persuasive.

> The greatest dissents do become court opinions and gradually over time their views become the dominant view. So that's the dissenter's hope: that they are writing not for today but for tomorrow.
> —NOTORIOUS RBG, aka Ruth Bader Ginsburg

I asked Sonoma County witch Dani Burlison, author of *Dendrophilia and Other Social Taboos* and editor of the zine *Lady Parts*, to show us another way to battle injustice with a jar—this time using repelling magic instead of sweetening magic. We think we should call them "sour pots" for all the piss and blood we're filling them with.

Sour Pots to Drown Injustice

DANI BURLISON

Historically, witch bottles—small glass or ceramic jars filled with sinister magical items like shards of glass, knotted thread, pins, rusted nails, hair, fingernail clippings, poisonous herbs, and bodily fluids—were used as protection against the evil doings of other witches. Spell casters would fill bottles with symbolic items of their choice and bury them in their yard, place them under floorboards, or hide them in walls or chimneys to ward off spells or evil spirits. The belief was that evil heading their way would get trapped in the bottle, tortured by the sharp things, poisoned by toxic herbs, eventually drowning in the bottle maker's urine, blood, or saliva.

Modern witches have reclaimed the magic of witch bottles; they make powerful, long-lasting spells when sealed up and buried, where they'll remain for years or, in some cases, centuries; a perfect way to cast spells for justice.

Gather

1 smallish glass or ceramic bottle or jar
with a tight-fitting lid

Rusty nails, pins, needles, pieces of broken glass

2–3 small mirrors to reflect bad deeds back on
person or institution this spell is against

1 foot or more of string or yarn for tying knots

1 dash of salt to neutralize any negative energy
not undone by the spell

2 or more small stones like black tourmaline or
smoky quartz to absorb any bad deeds or intentions
of the person or institution this spell is against

1 item of—or a symbol representing—the person
or organization that this spell is against

1 small cup of wine, saliva, or vinegar
(or all three if you really mean business!)

1 small strip of paper to write your spell on

Sharpie, paint, or blood to draw a sigil onto the bottle
(see the letter *S* for more on sigils)

Begin

Create sacred space by casting a circle and call in
the deities of your choice. For justice spells I call in
ancestors of resistance, rabble rousers of the past
that influence my activism, and I ask for protection and
assistance.

Repeat your intention three times with each item you place in the bottle. As I tie knots on the thread or yarn, I might say, "Let this knot bind white supremacists from doing harm in my community," or "May these mirrors reflect their hatred back unto them," or "May these nails bring justice to the rapist in my community."

Write your spell on a piece of paper, ending with "So Mote It Be" and insert it into the bottle last.

Seal the bottle. I might push pins into a cork, and I usually create a sigil for the spell and draw it onto the inside of the lid.

Bury the bottle. Pick a place far from your home, either in a forest or bog, maybe near a meeting place where the person or institution against whom your spell is working gather or work. (Think Nazi hangouts, a park where women, children and/or people of color are harassed, the neighborhood of a known abuser, the marching route of a white power parade.)

Remove any energy associated with the spell from your body. Take an Epsom salt bath, burn cedar, or light a cleansing candle.

Use any of your favorite protection spells or charms for you and your people to avoid backlash.

Proceed with Stealth

Before beginning magical work, it's wise to summon a sense of safety and protection from psychic negativity and real-world hate. You can be brave without making yourself needlessly vulnerable.

While I certainly don't believe in the devil, which is a postpagan invention, I've been privy to situations where a little salt, vinegar, and attentiveness could have gone a long way. Fires can start from candles left burning, unquiet spirits can show up and mess with our heads, or an ill-advised focus on a particular shitty sheriff can result in a psychic connection with said shitty sheriff—and that can be hard to break later.

Likewise, not everyone in this world responds well to the announcement that we are witches, and it's totally OK to keep a low profile sometimes and do what you need to do to protect yourself and your family from religious intolerance.

In art and dream may you proceed with abandon.
In life may you proceed with balance and stealth.
For nothing is more precious than the life force and
may the love of that force guide you as you go.
—PATTI SMITH

Some conjurers call upon their ancestors and appease them with offerings of things those ancestors liked in life. Some witches picture golden or silver light for protection. Some imagine hiding in the safety of darkness. Some visualize a cloak as a shield that will keep them safe from any weird energy that's floating around.

Many witches like to create a sacred space in which to cast their spells. It's like a little homemade postpatriarchal haven where we can be ourselves. To create your sacred haven, just tidy up the area where you're going to work and use visualization to see it as a comfortable place where good and healing things happen. It's often called "casting a circle" because we visualize its perimeter as a circle. (Witches like circles because we associate roundness with pussies and other common elements of femininity.) You can define the boundaries of your circle with salt, chalk, rocks, or a cord. (We use these props to focus our energy. When props are unavailable, improvise. Vivid visualization works just fine.)

You may also call the directions and incorporate anything that represents the elements associated with each direction. The Western tradition I was taught associates the north with the earth, the east with the air, the south with fire, and the west with water. The Eastern tradition I was taught associates the north with water, the east with wood, the south again with fire, the west with metal, and the center with earth. Whatever systems you use will become more powerful as you work with them.

Circle Tips to Stay Safe

- Bring any props you're going to use into your circle before you begin.

- State your intentions out loud.

- Stay inside the circle while you do your magical work.

- When you're finished, close your circle by thanking the directions, the elements, and any deities or spirits you invited in.

- If you've made an offering to ancestors or spirits, burn two white candles in front of the offering.

- Put candles out by covering the flame rather than by blowing them out.

- State your guiding ethos, such as "do no harm" or "don't be needlessly dickish."

- State that your circle is now closed.

- After your circle, wash your hands with salt-infused soap and carry on with your day.

Poplar Rose, a mystic, pole dancer, and hermit-witch, creator of the e-zine *we believe you: femmes surviving toxic masculinity,* has been a great teacher of mine when it comes to saying no and to staving off exhaustion. Under the rigid dichotomy of gender roles that is patriarchy, women and femmes are taught to selflessly take up the unpaid work of the society—from childcare to emotional labor. We're trained to remain in a constant state of burnout.

And that's intentional. Exhaustion separates us from our intuition. The patriarchy hopes we'll be too worn out to tap into our wisdom, and too beat down to rise up. At the same time, patriarchy normalizes abuse, telling us that everything from sexual assault to pay inequity is "just the way it is." It all becomes a devastating cycle: the patriarchy makes us its bitch, convincing us that injustice is inescapable and that we have to work tirelessly just to earn our right to be alive. To break this cycle, we need to prioritize self-care and boundaries.

I like using Poplar's elemental affirmations to call the directions and elements because she acknowledges all these truths. Try speaking each affirmation out loud as you hold a symbol of—or bring to mind—each element. Some examples of elemental symbols include a bowl of dirt in the north for earth, a bowl of water in the west, a yellow candle in the east for air, and a red candle or a cigarette in the south for fire.

You can experiment with swapping the *you* and *your* in these stanzas for *I* and *my* and see if you notice a difference.

Affirmations for Survivors

POPLAR ROSE

Earth

Your body is your own.

You are right sized.

You cannot be tarnished by another's touch.

What you did to survive in your body
was wise and necessary.

Being able to leave your body is a magical skill.

Deep breaths will bring you back,
when you are ready.

You are allowed to protect your home.

Seek nourishment.

You deserve to take up space.

Create a nest of safety.

Water

Your heart is your own.

It's OK to be broken.

Your messiness is sacred.

Your emotional labor is magic.

Your tears are setting you free.

You deserve to be loved: with caring
actions and sweet words.

Find people who will listen and believe.

You deserve loving witnesses who
want to see you heal.

You deserve to be held.

It's normal to miss the people who hurt you.

Fire

Your warmth is your own.

You choose whose hands are held at your hearth.

Your rage is sacred.

Your pain is fuel for your passion.

Your anger lights the way.

Go ahead, burn bridges.

Set your cage ablaze.

Your rage is a gift to keep you safe.

You deserve protection.

You are not responsible for the comfort of others.

Air

You deserve to be believed.

The people who believe you will make
themselves known.

The people who don't *don't deserve you*.

It matters how your story is told and who tells it.

It's normal to be confused about the details.

> What others believe does not define your story.
>
> Your story is a force of nature.
>
> You're allowed to hold a truth that is painful to someone else.
>
> You deserve to define yourself, on your terms.
>
> You are allowed to say good-bye to people who don't believe you.

Handy Provisional Initiation

Don't feel like you're a legit witch yet? Don't have any magical training or witchy ancestry that's known to you? It doesn't matter. Your first initiation can be very simple. It's just a commitment to step into your personal and spiritual strength and to use that strength to support and empower the marginalized and disarm those who abuse their power.

And yes, you can initiate yourself.

When

Initiate yourself during the full or waxing moon.

Gather

1 candle

1 necklace that represents your witchy self

Your intention

Begin

1. Cast your circle or create your sacred space. If you're with coven sisters, invite one another in.

2. Recite Poplar's affirmations on page 121, or dance to Earth, Wind & Fire.

3. Light the candle.

4. Look into its flame and say, *Count me in.*

5. Whether you're with others or alone, it's OK to be new at this.

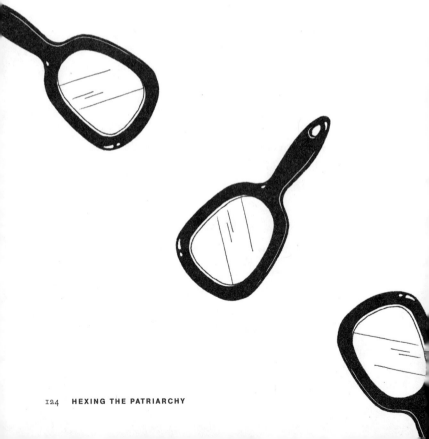

You know who you are.

You may not yet be able to envision a world beyond patriarchy, but you know that no person's power should require the subordination of another. You're ready to dust off your magic wand or make a new one.

You know that ceremony without action is often insufficient, but you know, too, that magic is vital to all deep and successful revolutions. The so-called leaders who have installed themselves in power are acting out the most grotesque archetypes of the toxic patriarch.

The compassionate, radical advocates we're rooting for have all their ancestors standing behind them, too. We're ready to see what power looks like when each of us is sovereign.

We've been burned, that's true. We have that in common. But we didn't die.

And now we're pulling the plug on their bullshit.

We're pulling the plug on our own bullshit, too. We're laying down the weapons of privilege. We're using our weapons of privilege *against* the enslavement machine.

The current system, reliant as it is on exploitation, will self-destruct, that's true.

But it's OK to give it an extra shove.

We are witches against the patriarchy, against white supremacy, and against economic exploitation.

If you can commit in your way to this effort, you are more than welcome here.

KICKBOXING

The letter *k* takes its shape from the open hand. We don't need to pick a fight, but magic isn't going to make *EVERYBODY* a sandwich. Talk to the hand. The hand says *STOP*. The hand will smack you if you don't stop.

Use Your Bare Hands And Feet To Vanquish Bro Culture And Explode The Gender Binary

One thing that sets femme-centric traditions apart from, say, most forms of Christianity, is that we think the body is cool. We like the flesh. We don't associate bleeding with impurity. And we sure as hell aren't going to sit around on some pedestal losing strength.

When I went to see a somatic therapist for my overactive anxiety, they recommended I should "do something that reminds you that you have a body. Take a walk or a hot shower—"

"Or do push-ups?" I'd once made a sweet little zine called *Push-Ups for the Revolution* to try and help us through ugly political times.

"Yes! Push-ups! Or eat."

Eat?

Even in the fairly feminist home I was raised in, when adolescence showed up in all its pimpled glory, I was scolded for eating too much. As if the "women's magazines" didn't already have me freaked out about my emerging belly.

In contrast, the boys of my generation—and the previous and the next—were encouraged to chow down. They'd be having contests to see who could gorge themselves on thirty hotdogs while we starved ourselves and purged. *Then the misogynists want to harp on the supposed physical inferiority of women and sparkly queerdos?*

They conspire to turn an entire gender into bonsai trees, and then they have the nerve to say, "Well, you're just not strong enough for the team, honey." It actually has a kind of twisted brilliance to it: imagine convincing your Olympic rivals that none of them should eat from the time they reach puberty until the day of the match. Talk about a fixed game.

Anyway, my somatic therapist said that eating not only nourished us, but it also served to ground us, too. As I bit into my dark chocolate bar that afternoon, I savored the moment, as yet another myth of the patriarchy melted in my mouth.

All this to say, magic can't be passive. We need to stay strong, whatever that means for our particular bodies. We need to eat. We need to move.

In the spirit of *push-ups*—and eating—*for the revolution*, I asked the kickboxers at Four Elements Fitness, a WOC-owned martial arts gym and art gallery in Oakland, to share their magic. They sent this group-authored spell.

Kickboxing Hex to Vanquish Bro Culture and Explode the Gender Binary

FOUR ELEMENTS FITNESS

Begin

Put on your workout clothes.
They might be black or tie-dyed
Or have leather or fringe
Or sequins.

■

Warm-Up

Read Audre Lorde, Cherrie Moraga.

Do fifty burpees to get strong.

Read Kate Bornstein, Leslie Marmon Silko.

Fifty more burpees
(Only if you want to. Take a break whenever you need.)

■

Strength Training

Steal the single-sex bathroom sign
From a restaurant with stairs and no ramps.

Attach it to one of those Joe Rogan kettlebells
That looks like an angry monkey.

Throw it in the deepest part of Lake Merritt.
(Don't get the water on you. It's polluted.)

■

Stretching

Ask the guy who said,
You kick pretty well for a girl
To hold up twenty dollars from his wallet.

He will hold it too high for your fists to reach.

Use your feet to kick it
Into 100 pieces.

If he looks upset, let him keep 83 of them,
Or 62 of them if you are a woman of color.

■

Striking

Jab, to silence your comments about my body.

Jab, don't get cross when I call you out.

Jab, cross, not letting you off the hook.

Jab, cross, hook, up yours.

Jab, cross, hook, uppercut, kick
You out of positions of power.

■

Grappling

Tell your pronouns to an attractive stranger.

Pummel mercury until it becomes gold.

■

Cooldown

Wring out your sports bra.

Collect the sweat in a pepper spray can.

Shoot it at the first guy who tries
To block your path as you walk home.

Take deep breaths of cool night air
through your nose.

■

Recovery

Light a fire in your toaster.

Burn a YouTube comment that says,
Make me a sandwich.

Then make yourself a sandwich
With herbs you grew in the dirt of your windowsill,
And eat it. You need the nourishment
Of Mother Earth.

■

If you were catcalled during the day,
Go to sleep with your face on a cat.

If you are allergic to cats, a person,
Stuffed animal, or dog who doesn't worry about
Being called a bitch
Will also work.

■

LUNAR LOVE

The runic *L*, Laguz,
meaning water, the source
of life, signifies both flow
and potential impasse.
Moon magic can help.

Ally Yourself With The Moon, Who Did Not Appreciate That Colonial Flag-Planting Crap

Moon gazing is so central to femme-centric magic that the patriarchs even found a way to gaslight us linguistically, calling our worship lunacy and calling us lunatics whenever they couldn't control us.

The most conspicuous term for insanity in nineteenth-century American and British law, the word *lunatic* was officially removed from US federal law when the House and Senate passed legislation and Barack Obama signed on the dotted line on December 28, 2012—a full moon.

I guarantee you there was some moon magic in action to secure that reversal.

If you're just getting started working with lunar magic, try getting a calendar that tracks the moon's cycle and just jotting down how you're feeling each day, noting major events or inspirations and marking any patriarchal shenanigans you notice in your daily life or in the larger political sphere. After a few months, go back through your notes, comparing your feelings and what was going on for you to the particular phase of the moon on that day. See if you notice any patterns.

There are a million different ways to work with the moon—across hundreds of different traditions and possibilities—but in the traditions I work with, we say that the new moon is the time to start new projects and set new intentions.

The waxing moon—from the moment after the moon is new to when it's full—is an auspicious time for pushing productivity and doing work and spells to amplify all the good things. If there's something you want to *increase*, like the number of progressive queers and women of color in government, cast a spell for it during the waxing moon.

The full moon is lucky for concentrating on magical work that needs extra power—so it's also a good time to meet up with our coven sisters or other witchy buddies for group rituals to, say, take back the Supreme Court from its rapey, misogynist judges and concentrate on the continuing good health of our allies on the bench.

During these full moon rituals, whether we're alone or together, it's fitting to make offerings to our ancestors or deities to thank them for their continued support. If you've been feeling strengthened by your great-grandmother's spirit, make her a cake she would have had on a special occasion where she grew up. Put a slice on your altar for her, and enjoy the rest with your coven—or just with your cat. If Mary Magdalene has been inspiring your confidence, make her some red Easter eggs.

The waning moon—from the moment after it's full until the next new moon—is a restorative time, opportune for self-care, teaching and disseminating information, cleansing, downsizing, and casting spells against things we want to *decrease*. So it's time to banish evil influences, neutralize enemies, and reduce harm—basically, time to hex the patriarchy. Wash your hair and watch The Man fall out.

Finally, the dark moon—the time when the moon is not visible at all, just before the new moon—is excellent for introspection and prophecy but also for dealing with attackers and enacting justice. The dark moon is a beautiful time to do rituals to banish addictions as well as to say "enough is enough" to the white-boy power structure hell bent on destruction. Try this quick ritual—courtesy of Vajra Conjure Wright:

Dark Moon Spell

Gather

1 black candle

Mineral oil

Cayenne pepper

Begin

1. Write on the candle that which you'd like to get rid of.

2. Dress the candle with mineral oil and sprinkle it with cayenne pepper.

3. Say,

> *Dark moon dark moon come on quick*
> *Burn these suckers because they're sick*
> *Burn them all the way down*
> *Boom.*

Whether or not timing your magic with the moon becomes your thing, try paying a little more attention to the moon in the sky and allowing the silvery light to remind you to open yourself up to your own intuition.

Los Angeles–based feminist designer Sarah Faith Gottes-diener, author of the cult classic *Many Moons* workbooks and the *Moonbeaming* newsletter, says, "I always felt like I was a little different. I had a hard time of it until I stepped into my intuition, decided to truly love myself, and trust the messages coming through."

So let's make a moon-shaped embroidery of this Sarah-inspired to-do list:

Step into intuition
Love self
Trust messages

Then, do Sarah's spell to protect the moon, even if it sometimes feels like the world is careening toward certain doom.

Spell to Protect the Moon

SARAH FAITH GOTTESDIENER

There's no more effective hex to the patriarchy than living in a way that resists and subverts it. Our earliest calendars were lunar, and our present-day one still reflects this wheel of the year. Moontime—the cycle that follows the moon—is feminist and infinite, envisioning time as spiral rather than linear. It follows the natural rhythms of inspiration and seed planting; growth, fullness, and abundance; decay, death, and rebirth. It rebels against the idea that capitalism, production, extraction, greed, isolation, and competition are the ways in which we define success.

This spell honors and protects the moon and in doing so empowers our hearts and keeps us hydrated.

When

Full moon, but any time will work,
if the intention is aligned.

Gather

1 bowl of filtered water

Moonstone, selenite, rose quartz (optional)

3 clear drinking glasses

Candles or tea lights

Begin

1. Place the bowl of filtered water outside or by a window that catches moonlight. You may wish to put any water-safe crystals in the bowl to charge the water. Leave the water outside for at least thirty minutes.

2. Set your altar up with your drinking glasses and your candles.

3. Go outside if you can, or by a moon-viewing window.

4. Ground yourself and cast your circle.

5. Spend time connecting with the moon. Open your eyes wide and have a staring contest with her. Close your eyes and see if any images present themselves. Listen for any messages that want to come up from inside you. If able, plant your legs wide, and lift your arms up so that you become a pentacle. Feel the energy of the moonlight

cascading into your body. Connect with the energy inside you: energy that is your own, and energy that is a gift of the cosmos.

6. Take your moon water bowl and go inside to your altar.

7. Pour the water carefully into the three glasses. Put them on the altar.

8. Light your candles.

9. Say: *I vow to protect you, Moon. I vow to protect myself.*

10. Drink one glass of water.

11. Say: *I show frequent appreciation of the moon. I give myself constant gratitude. I promise to love the moon inside of me. I promise to keep my heart open.*

12. Drink another glass of water.

13. Say: *I honor the sacredness of the moon. I honor the sacredness in all of us. So it is. All this or better. Blessed be.*

14. Drink the third glass of water.

15. After you put the last glass of water down, give thanks. Thank the moon for being your guide. Thank your guides, teachers, ancestors, and all the other moonbeamers—all those other talking animals that live on moontime. Spells become amplified in this way.

16. As the candle light flickers, as the moon water enters your system, let yourself breathe. You are yourself now, you are the moon, and you are also everyone else who are themselves and who are also the moon. Let yourself be. Sing, chant, or say any words you need to express. Write down any wishes, dreams, or visions that have come up.

17. Close your circle. You may wish to keep your candle burning through the night if it's in a safe spot.

MONEY MAGIC

The letter *M* takes
its shape from the waves
of *LA MAR*, the sea.
Surf the waves of
economic liberation.

BURN DOWN CAPITALISM
AND IN ITS ASHES PLANT THE SEEDS
OF A SOLIDARITY ECONOMY

All precapitalist societies believed in magic.

Then debt and shame inspired the European conquests that would begin to implement capitalism around the globe. (Spanish conquistador and Aztec Empire destroyer Hernán Cortés was a gambling addict who borrowed for his trip and made the ultimate, psychotic gamble.)

The ensuing history of colonization, a globalized slave trade, white supremacy, increasing misogyny, land alienation, and the dissing of magic are intimately intertwined.

The witch hunts, a mostly female genocide, helped create an exploitable proletariat working class for the rise of capitalism. (When wealthy male tyrants complain about "witch hunts," call bullshit.) The criminalization of poverty came next (still a relatively recent event in human history). The capitalist state seeks to control women's reproductive rights every time they want to control the supply and demand of various classes of labor. All this to say: capitalism has to go. We all know that. The entire monetary system will probably have to go.

Take inspiration. On Halloween in 1968, an activist group calling itself Women's International Terrorist Conspiracy from Hell (W.I.T.C.H.) emerged in New York City. Dressed in pointy hats and black capes, women carried their brooms into the financial district and chanted "Wall Street, Wall Street, up against the Wall Street," causing the stock market to make an unexpected and welcome downturn. Soon, radical W.I.T.C.H. covens sprang up around the United States and as far away as Japan, targeting sexist universities, beauty pageants, and bridal expos. The movement was antihierarchical to the point of anarchy—which is just the way many of us witches like things—and favored flash-mob-like public actions.

Because capitalism, patriarchy, and all the elements that conspire to keep women poor are so insidiously intertwined, we need to come at it from every angle—transferring resources from the rich back to the poor and building a new solidarity economy or, perhaps more apropos, a coven economy.

So let's do some money magic for joyful survival and for the healing of debt and shame—because, once that wound heals, the virus that is capitalism just won't be able to get in.

Now, I want you to think about money energy and how money has worked in your life and in your communities. The instinct of money, like water, is to flow. Where has it been flowing in your world? When we're working money magic, the goal is to activate the flow in direction of equitable abundance rather than for the magnification of already toxic power.

If you ever think to yourself, *But where will the money come from?* answer your own question with confidence: *The money will come from wherever it is right now.* And where it is right now is with a bunch of primarily white and male capitalist con artists. Practice visualizing, in vivid detail, money literally traveling from the bank accounts of the 1 percent into the bank accounts of the 99.

Begin tithing money or making secular reparations—any percentage of what you bring in—to your teachers, to agents of change, and to people robbed and made vulnerable by the current system.

And remember to use the rest of the money that passes through your hands to support radical, cooperative, and independent endeavors.

In these ways, we redirect the flow.

In my own workings with money magnetism, I've noticed that money doesn't seem to be attracted to desperate need but rather to an air of casual wealth. So, before we begin any cash-conjuring spell for ourselves or our communities, we've got to assume a neutral, nonaggressive attitude of regal entitlement. Capitalism has taught us to feel unworthy, so we shake that off. Patriarchy has taught us that we don't deserve to be paid for our work, so we spit that bullshit back in the patriarchy's face.

Spine straight.
Do a quick self-worth reset.

Your value has nothing to do with whether or not the capitalist war machine likes your smile.

Say to yourself, "I am the queen of my world. I have as much right to be here as the stars and the dirt."

Then try this spell to keep the money flowing at home:

Money-Flowing Spell

Gather

3 silver coins
Salt water
Bowl
Milk (cow, soy, hemp, or other)
Shovel or other digging tool

Begin

1. Let three silver coins sit and cleanse in a bowl of salt water for two days.

2. Dig a hole to bury your coins somewhere near your front door. I like to choose a place I step over or across each day as I come and go, but burying them in a small potted plant near the door will work just as well.

3. Pour a little fresh milk over the coins before you cover them up with dirt.

4. Leave them buried for at least six weeks.

5. If you like, you may dig up the coins after the six weeks and carry them with you, or you may leave them in the dirt. Either way, the money is flowing.

A friend who leaves supplies for migrants in the Arizona desert has started burying charged coins in this fashion so that all who step across the US border may find prosperity here or wherever their paths take them. May we all heal from capitalism, as well, and leave behind the legacy of shame and debt that gave rise to it.

Erica Feldmann, the head witch in charge of HausWitch Home and Healing, the coolest intersectional feminist magic shop in Salem, Massachusetts, works in what she calls a coven economy. She credits her wildly successful business—where she sells magical cleaning supplies and spell kits for everything from finding a home and making it cozy to dominating the whole fucking world—to the support of her coven sisters. And it's my kind of coven: "all different kinds of weirdos that just kind of click together." They support one another financially, sharing skills and hooking each other up with paid gigs.

She offers this spell for releasing and healing from capitalism.

Witches, Workers, Humans Unite! Spell

ERICA FELDMANN

When

Perform this spell in the last few minutes before
the new moon so that you begin the spell during the
most powerful time for banishing and finish it
during the most powerful time for rebirth.

Gather

1 small black candle

1 small white candle

1 small candle in any color you like

Tower tarot card

Star tarot card

Ace of pentacles tarot card
(you will need to sacrifice this card
so a photocopy will do)

Pen

Ammonite fossil
(a spiral-shaped shell fossil)

Begin

1. Hold the black candle and meditate for a moment on the
   harm that late-stage capitalism is bringing to the planet.
   Call in any specific imagery or examples that you feel
   personally attached to. Light the black candle and place
   it on top of the tower card.

2. Hold the white candle and meditate for a moment on the power of the masses overcoming the power of the few. Imagine the oppressive chains of a profit-driven world simply melting away like the wax of the candle. Light the white candle from the black candle and place it on top of the star card.

3. Once the black candle is almost burnt out, and the moon has become new, hold the colored candle and meditate for a moment on a world where everyone has equal access to resources and the ability to survive and thrive, a world healed of the harm capitalism has caused. Light the colored candle from the white candle and say these words aloud or to yourself:

> Capitalism's time has come.
> I call for an evolution.
> Collaboration over competition.
> People over profit.
> Empathy over exploitation.
> Sustainability over scarcity.
> In solidarity with all of Earth's people.

4. With your colored candle burning, write out "solidarity economy" in a spiral pattern on your ace of pentacles card to mimic your ammonite. Place it under the colored candle.

5. Hold your ammonite and meditate on the possibilities of what comes next. Our fossil reminds us that there was a time before capitalism and there will be a time after, that time is not linear and everything is cyclical.

6. Let your colored candle burn all the way down, covering the card in wax.

7. Finish by burying the card and the shell in the ground, planting the seed for a new world.

NEVER ERASE

The letter *N*—embodying
every no—comes to
us from the snake of
Egyptian hieroglyphs. It
shape-shifted into the
Arabic letter *NUN*, which
means fish, and then
shape-shifted again.
Both snakes and fish are
symbols of the Goddess, of
transformation, of fertility,
and of freedom seeking.

Raze The Border Walls To The Ground: No Person Is "Illegal"

The tools of oppression begin with the stories we're told—and the stories we tell ourselves. One of the ways the patriarchy stays in power is by convincing us that "it's always been this way." They banish our artists to museum basements, marginalize our religions as superstition, reframe our legit DIY health care as old wives' tales, and erase our powerful predecessors from our history books.

There's a reason not many of us know the biographies of

- China's female ruler, Wu Zetian
- Empress Theodora of Byzantium
- Nur Jahan of Mughal
- Radical nun Hildegard of Bingen
- Sybil Ludington, heroine of the Revolutionary War who rode farther than Paul Revere
- Trans spy and diplomat Chevalier d'Eon
- Sculptor Edmondia Lewis
- Rebecca Latimer, the first woman to serve in the Senate

- Activists Sylvia Rivera and Marsha P. Johnson, founders of the Gay Liberation Front
- Shirley Chisolm, the first Black woman to run for president of the United States

And it's not that we're dumbbells. It's that the patriarchs who wrote and published our textbooks didn't *want us to know*. With feminist pressure in the 1970s, mainstream historians threw in a few interesting white women, further whitewashed those women's politics and power, and called it updated.

We're not falling for that.

It's still just *his* story.

Instead, let's uncover the histories of the radical femme and female leaders who inspired our foremothers and kept the fires of revolution burning.

Let's disarm the patriarchy by saying no to our own erasure.

Let's start by remembering Teresa Urrea.

Like most saints, Teresa was an incredibly complicated person. Born in 1873, the girl who would become the Saint of Cabora spent the first half of her childhood with her mother, an indigenous single teen parent, and the second half of her childhood with her father, the wealthy rancher whom her mother worked for. Like many of her contemporary northern Spiritualists of the late 1800s, a childhood illness brought on her early visions and spiritual power.

Back from the near-death experience, Teresa became a revolutionary preacher who drew the wrath of the Catholic Church by insisting that priests weren't necessary intermediaries and the panic of the Mexican dictatorship by inspiring resistance fighters. She was exiled to the United States in 1892. As a curandera, she never charged the poor for her medical services, but as a woman with a family to support in a capitalist world, she took her healing powers on a road show for a pharmaceutical company in the early 1900s.

Michelle Threadgould, an Oakland-based Latinx journalist who explores intersections between art, brujería, and *curanderismo,* offers up this prayer in honor of Teresa Urrea to say *no* to erasure. Channeled for undocumented people and women of color in particular, it's a prayer to recite whenever we're feeling disregarded. It's an intention not to be forgotten—applying Mexican folk healing as a starting point.

A Prayer for Those Without a Prayer

MICHELLE THREADGOULD

I remember the Mexican folk saint Teresa Urrea. She was a curandera and folk healer revered for her ability to heal with her hands and to channel the dead to perform miracles. Records show that she healed thousands and was known as Santa Teresa de Cabora. In fact, she was so powerful, the Mexican dictator Porfirio Diaz was afraid of her influence. He banished her to the United States, and her followers, the Caboristas, waged a war in her name against tyranny, against patriarchy, against all that breaks the spirit and turns it into dust.

Like Teresa, we are all *cajitas*—or vessels—of hopes and dreams and human spirit. Let us see these spirits. Let us stand alongside them. Let us support them.

Begin

1. Say this once with your hand on your heart: *You will never erase me.*

   It's a prayer I find myself repeating. I think of the undocumented immigrants living hidden in churches: the underground railroad of today. I think of the people afraid to go to school, to hospitals, or to work, for fear of being deported.

2. Say this three times with your eyes closed: *You will never destroy us.*

   The first time, hiss it. The second time, spit it. The third time, surrender it.

3. Reach down, touch the earth, and whisper to the plants:

   > *I belong here.*
   > *Su espíritu pertenece aquí.*
   > *We all belong here.*
   > *Your roots are my roots.*

4. Take a handful of soil, make a fist. Think of what Earth would be like without the presence of patriarchy. Without *dueños* (owners). Without fear. Without hate.

5. Blow on the soil, until there is no anger or rancor left.

6. Fold your hands and pray: *Thank you, Teresa. We will never be erased.*

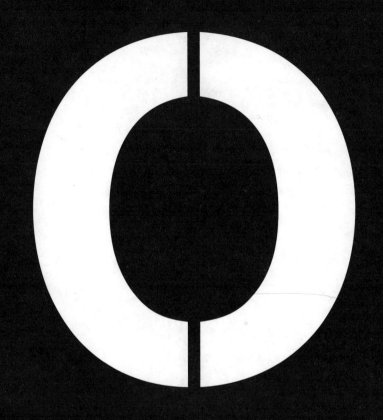

OFFERING

O comes from the
Phoenician letter *EYN*,
meaning "eye."
Make art from your
visions day and night.

Make Gifts For Ancestors And Deities To Repay Them For Their Hard Work Punching Misogynists In The Throat

When we ask spirit for assistance—whether we're petitioning an ancestor to fix our kids' schools or invoking Artemis, the queer goddess of the hunt, to speed up an impeachment—it's a good idea to make an offering or the promise of an offering once the work is complete. I mean, what's in it for Grandma? Would she like a candle, incense, water, flowers, or the green chile tamales she loved?

As magic makers, we often don't *worship* spirits so much as we *work with* them, so we might even ask the spirit what they'd like by way of payment. Obviously, if they want the neighbor's cat, we'll say no! But usually it's nothing like that. They've had a long day, and they just want some kombucha. My stepfather, John, for example, who is now in spirit, has gladly sneaked into publishing offices on my behalf and opened doors the patriarchy wanted to keep closed to me—all for a little peanut brittle on his altar.

Some magicians say that our spirits have gone so long without feeding that any offering made with heart supercharges our magic. It can't hurt to experiment! See what happens when you make a delicious pasta puttanesca for your Italian Strega Nona, pour a ritual shot of rum for Elegua, do a dance for Emma Goldman, or pick blue flowers from your garden for Marie Laveau.

Maman Brigitte, the Afro-Irish saint of graveyards, passion, justice, and fertility, is known to love candles and pepper-infused rum. If you need healing, honor her:

Cocktail for Maman Brigitte

Gather

½ teaspoon peppercorns

1 ounce rum

Drawing supplies (paper and pencil)

1 black candle

Begin

1. Make some pepper-infused rum by simply putting the peppercorns in a mason jar and adding the rum. Let the concoction sit for a day or two at room temperature.

2. Spend some time drawing a picture of what you imagine Maman Brigitte might look like. Put her portrait on your altar. Draw an elm tree or a weeping willow, and put that on the altar next to her.

3. Light the candle for her and talk with her about the healing you're seeking. You might ask for healing help for anything from a more physically manifesting disease, like breast cancer, to a broader societal ill, like racial discrimination in our court system.

4. Offer her a shot of your homemade pepper-infused rum by placing the drink in front of her portrait.

5. Promise to make her a lemon poppy-seed cake with butter rum sauce when the healing is complete. (Of course, you'll remember to deliver!)

6. Thank Maman Brigitte in advance for her help.

Anna Doogan, one of my favorite Portland storytellers, weaves tales about floral prescriptions for loneliness and secret covens on misty cliffs. She inherited a witchy lineage from her mother. "I was raised with a quiet type of magic," she tells me. "With great regularity, my mother took us outside to get energy from the moon, drove to various shops to collect bundles of sweet-smelling herbs and candles, and kept a library stocked with books about the powers of plants, flowers, dreams, and visualization. I can still remember full moon summer nights, damp and sticky with humidity, stretched out in the grass in the backyard, arms stretched towards the sky, taking it all in."

Now Anna couples her magic with art, dance, and activism. "Dismantling such a deeply destructive system built on patriarchy and supremacy will take a force," she says, "but *it can be done*. I believe this. Let *that* be our intention."

She gifts us with this highly adaptable ritual for offering our creative energy and artifacts to the spirits.

Spell for Momentum:
Offerings of Art and Noise

ANNA DOOGAN

When

This spell is best performed after sunset, when you'll have some quiet and stillness for working.

Gather

Jasmine

Rosemary

Sage

Jar or bowl

1 candle

Incense (optional)

Vinegar

Garlic

Silver paper

Pen or pencil

A creative offering
(a song, a painting)

Prepare

Set yourself up in a comfortable softly lit room. Moonlight is also lovely. No need to wait for a full moon or magical timing, as time is of the essence in dismantling our toxic and pervasive white supremacist patriarchy.

Before beginning, harvest jasmine, rosemary, and sage to ward off negative energy. Wear what makes you feel comfortable and powerful in your skin. Wearing nothing is fine, too. Anything that allows freedom of movement and enough stretchiness to smash dominant systems of power, privilege, and oppression.

Begin

1. Place the herbs in the bowl where you can see and smell them. Surround yourself with some green plants you've nurtured as well.

2. Light the candle and some incense, if you like, to create a mood.

3. Sprinkle vinegar and garlic in the corners of the room you are in, lest any unchecked misogyny tries to come seeping in from outside.

4. Cut a silver piece of paper into the shape of a revolution.

5. Cut a second piece of paper into the sound of momentum.

6. Now, write your intentions on the pieces of paper:

   For the destruction of the current paradigm.

   For the safety and protection of all marginalized people and populations.

For the empowerment of all who have been shamed, devalued, harassed, targeted, slurred, objectified, harmed, and silenced in their identities.

Let our uprising now frighten those in power.

7. Add your own words to personalize the petition.

8. Following this, send your intentions out to the world by burning them in the candle flame, or plant them in your garden alongside the vegetable seeds. (If you're feeling particularly crafty, stitch the words into a small dream pillow with a handful of dried rosehips.)

9. Now, make your creative offering, whatever it may be— and make some noise. Let your voice become an offering. Shouting is fine, or singing. If you're a writer, read one of your pieces aloud, at full volume. Hear your voice echo off walls. If you're a musician, play your instrument. If you haven't an instrument, dance. Let your body tell its story. Paint a picture and present it to your altar. Take up as much space as possible. Make no apologies for it.

Say out loud:
May we fight the patriarchy.
May we knock it all down.
May we lift and empower the voices of others.
May we scream over those who try to quiet us.

10. When you're finished, take a long rest. Enjoy some of your favorite things to eat and drink. Tea, wine, and cake are all delicious options. Listen to your favorite music. Take a nap and dream new dreams.

11. Make a small sachet of home-grown lavender and refusal to be shamed or silenced. Tie it all with a piece of twine. Carry it in your pocket to remember.

12. Repeat as needed.

POPPETS

The seventeenth letter
of the Hebrew alphabet,
PEH, represents the open
mouth and, by extension,
word and expression—
the power of language
and silence. We are
learning when to speak
truth to power and when
to remain inscrutable.

Make A Dolly Of An Entitled Rapist Who Has The Nerve To Threaten Our Right To Control Our Own Bodies And Stick Pins In Him

A poppet is a doll—or a little puppet, as the word suggests—that we make to represent a person, and then we use that doll to either neutralize or help the person it represents.

The first time I used a poppet was to help a friend escaping a domestic violence situation.

I made two dolls. The first doll represented my friend, and I sewed a sprig of rosemary for protection into the hem of her shirt and piece of a rose quartz to represent her precious heart. The other doll represented her abuser, and I filled that one with piss, glass shards, cayenne, and Lysol.

My friend needed to get out of the bad scene—that was the first priority—but if possible, she needed to keep the family apartment and just get him out. So while she went through the process of getting a move-out order and a restraining order, I worked with the two dolls.

First, I wrote her address on a piece of paper and put that under her doll.

Then, I lit a rainbow-layered seven-day candle for home cleansing, and every morning, I moved his doll a little farther away from her doll—and farther from the address where she intended to stay.

Once the abuser doll was safely out of hitting range, I wrapped him up and flushed him down the toilet.

Then I got in the shower and salt-scrubbed myself *real* good.

Doreen Valiente, the British mother of modern witchcraft, wasn't formally initiated as a witch until she was an adult. But as a kid she "had the sight," as they say. By age thirteen, in 1935, she'd learned about sympathetic magic, herbalism, and poppet making—probably from that greatest of witch schools, the public library.

And here's her first poppet story: Doreen's single mom worked as a housekeeper and complained that a colleague kept picking on her. Doreen instructed her mother to get a lock of the woman's hair, which she did. Doreen then made a figurine of the woman, wound the woman's hair around the doll, and, using traditional herbs and black-ended pins, cast a spell to protect her mother.

Soon enough, a blackbird showed up at the house where Doreen's mother worked, and this bird harassed the bully by tapping on the window every time she entered a room and following her around the house, pecking at all the windows. The bullying ended.

Michelle Tea is an award-winning memoir author, anthology editor, literary organizer, and author of *Modern Tarot: Connecting with Your Higher Self through the Wisdom of the Cards*. The first time I met Michelle she was reading tarot cards at a lesbian bar in San Francisco. It must have been the mid-1990s because everybody was still drinking. I asked her to pull a single card for me, and she presented me with the empress.

"Ah," she said, "you're the earth mother. Your connections run deep."

When Michelle's higher self wants to hex the patriarchy, she turns to poppets.

Now, I already mentioned using urine in my own poppet. And Michelle is going to echo that here, calling for menstrual blood if your body makes it. Using body fluids in magic is old school and found in traditions from those noted in Greek mythology to Sicilian *strega* to the old German witches to American Hoodoo. It's one of those things Puritan and Victorian patriarchal culture taught us was too icky to touch—or even talk about!—but I think if you try it, you'll find that it's a powerful magical tool. There's a reason they want us to stay away from it. Hell, the Nordic god Thor femmed-up his power by bathing in a whole *river* of menstrual blood. If Thor can handle a river, I think we can handle a few drops.

Poppin'

MICHELLE TEA

Poppets are more familiar to many folks as the Voodoo dolls of Afro-Caribbean traditions, but they were also used throughout Europe and can be a great hexing tool for today's witches fighting the patriarchy worldwide.

It might gross you out to have to make a little doll of the little man who's trying to crush your glory. If so, grab some fabric and make something that signifies his realm of power or the patriarchy itself. I personally like the specificity of a poppet that looks just like the most powerful patriarch we're dealing with on a given day, so if you can manage it, do it!

Now, stay with me. We're going to work with menstrual blood, if this is something your body makes. Menstrual blood has a lot of power, especially because the patriarchy has made it their kryptonite. If your body doesn't make menstrual blood, use urine—or a little semen if your body makes it. Body fluids are powerful and demonized by the patriarchy even though they are all holy and natural.

Gather

Fabric

Paint

Cotton

Pepper (black or red)

Garlic

Pine needles

1 egg

1 cinnamon stick

Quartz, amethyst, or jet stone (optional)

Needle and thread

Body fluids (any amount, from a drop to a splash to a bowlful, of menstrual blood, piss, or semen)

Epsom salt

A few drops of eucalyptus oil

Mint-infused water, frankincense resin, or the energy-cleanser of your choice

Rose quartz (optional)

Begin

1. Make your poppet. You don't need great skills to sew this dolly; it can be as crude as he is. Paint it orange and call it a day. Stuff it with cotton, and also with pepper, garlic, and pine needles. Smash an egg and stuff the shell in there. A cinnamon stick is good. Add some quartz or amethyst or jet if you like. Then sew the thing up.

2. Soak a cord, rope, ribbon, or piece of string in your fluid of choice, and wrap your poppet with it, essentially tying it up. Talk to it as you go. You can craft your own spell, like: *Forces of queer pagan feminism and the holy Earth and all the universe, prevent this being from doing harm, weaken his energy and his power and the energy and power of his followers.* Or you can just be like: *You fucking scumbag, leave immigrants alone, leave people of color alone, leave Mexico alone, leave trans people alone, leave poor people alone, leave Earth alone, leave women alone, leave sick people alone, leave queer people alone, etc., etc., forever.*

3. Take this poppet and bury it deeply somewhere you're confident it will not be disturbed. If such a place does not exist near you, put it in a box and leave it in your basement, attic, garage, or closet until the tired old ideology it represents passes into whatever world comes next, hopefully to receive his karmic comeuppance.

4. After spending so much time thinking of this cruel, corrupt person and the misery they're sowing, you might be feeling sort of yucky. End this spell with a cleansing ritual. Take a bath in water heavily doused with Epsom salt and a few drops of eucalyptus oil. Spritz the air around you with the mint-infused water or burn the frankincense or otherwise engage the energetic cleanser of your choice. Sit with a rose quartz, and realign yourself with the powerful love that motivated you to make the poppet in the first place. Feel yourself bathed in love and light, and shoot it back into the world from your solar plexus.

Good work, witches!

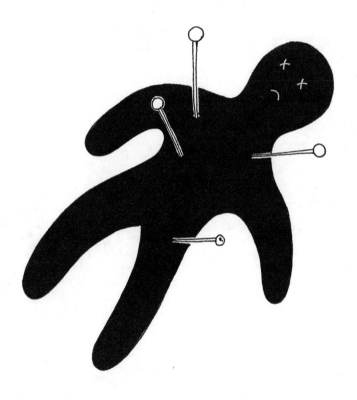

QUILTING

Three thousand years ago,
the letter Q sounded like
$QOPH$, and it represented
a ball of yarn. You can
still see the yarn, rolled
up with a knitting needle,
ready to be fashioned into
something powerful.

REFRAME "WOMEN'S WORK" IN THE CONTEXT OF A TOTAL TAKEDOWN OF THE PATRIARCHY

Have you already noticed that this book is built like a quilt? Different witches and magical practitioners and growers of plants and music makers and fighters have each contributed a square. I've sewn them together with batting and backing.

Repeating patterns begin to emerge.

Step back and you see a broader pattern still.

We're here to reframe "women's work" in the context of a total fucking takedown of the patriarchy.

American quilting originated with the early industrial revolution—a historical shitshow that at once made fabrics more affordable and turbo-powered the patriarchal project, leaving women scrambling to record our histories in forms the boss men wouldn't find threatening. The slave chain and Texas tears patterns were created and adapted in response to escalating conflict and resistance to enslavement. Escape routes were sewn into quilted cloth. Coded blocks were used on quilts, which were hung outside, signaling that a house was a safe place to stop on the Underground Railroad, that secret network of

We are the ones
who make things, and
make things happen.
—PAM GROSSMAN,
What Is a Witch

people offering shelter and help to enslaved people escaping from the South into northern free states and Canada in the nineteenth century.

As migrant crises escalate, I wonder what secret signals we'll develop to communicate solidarity and support.

As we get to know real witches—not just the stereotypes put on Halloween cards and in our heads—we notice that many don't follow elaborate traditions but rather have one or a few practices they use for meditation, conjuring, self-care, and activism. We notice that as they get older, more and more of their art making and seemingly everyday tasks carry the intentional energy of magic. It's not just something they do on Friday or Saturday nights.

Sailor Holladay, writer, teacher, and quilter living on unceded Kalapuya land in Oregon, is adept at making power from scraps. She's sewing hexagons for the revolution, making our work visible.

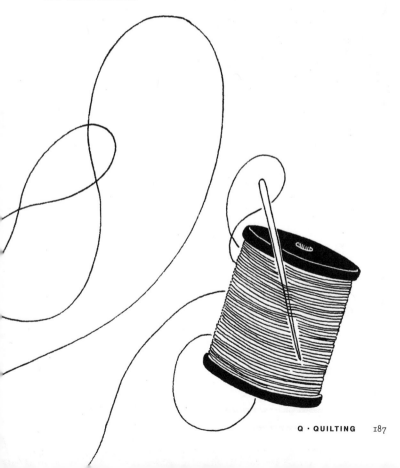

Labor Made Visible Quilt

SAILOR HOLLADAY

Let's make a quilt of hexagons, those six-sided shapes that together make up a honeycomb, the storage unit of hard-working honeybees.

Gather

Cotton, linen, or silk
(about three times the yardage you'll
want your finished quilt to be)

Needle

Thread

Hindsight

Regret

Desire for change

Patience

Time

Prepare

I invite you to cut pieces of fabric and sew them into a pattern that pleases you. It's time to cut your life in pieces on purpose and stitch it back together. This time in your image. The patience you have had with how slowly things change toward the better will come in handy here.

Begin

1. Thread the needle.

2. Cut your fabric and begin to stitch. Push the needle through the fabric. You are the needle: up, down, up, down, up. Make your stitches as short or long as you like. The stitching will take a long time. The hours it takes to make these hexagons are the months it takes to make this quilt. The months it takes to make this quilt are an acknowledgment of the beauty you find in your invisible labor. This quilt is your labor made visible.

3. With each stitch say, *My labor is my own. I make my world for myself.* An invisible mender you are no more.

No other person will know how long this quilt took you, but this quilt will know, and you will keep this quilt and it will remind you: "You have kept me to account for your labor. You have kept me because you made me, and I am beautiful."

How long it took isn't what it's about. You'll find out what it's about by hour twenty. That will change by hour fifty.

Like the women before you, and the women before those women, when you feel groundless, hopeless, aimless, there is a place to return to in the making of this quilt.

Once complete, you won't give this quilt to anyone. You'll give it to yourself to remind you of your willingness to fall apart, your desire for change, and your ability to make your world in a way that pleases you.

R

RECLAIMING
POWER

The runic ᚱ, or Reid,
is a ride—any journey
that leads to change.

Call On The Goddess Of Transformation To Do No Harm And Take No Shit

The first self-identified witches I met as an adult were part of the Reclaiming tradition, a nonhierarchical affiliation of sometimes self-initiated magicians inspired in the late 1970s and 1980s by the likes of Diane Baker and author Starhawk. Combining the Goddess movement with social justice activism, Reclaiming was and is both political and spiritual. Faced with nuclear annihilation—not to mention giant shoulder pads and acid-washed jeans—these progressive, ecofeminist witches sought a cosmic do-over. They wanted to reclaim, revise, recenter, and reject the powerful's definition of our reality.

I like to think of reclaiming both in the context of a rediscovery of marginalized religious practices and a psychic retrieval of the energy the patriarchy has bled from us.

To learn a new kind of spell for reclaiming, I paid a visit to my rock-star friend, a second-generation West Coast witch, Rhiannon Flowers.

When I first met Rhiannon on a rainy Portland day back in the early 2000s, she went by Dexter. She'd named herself, like so many of us do when we're ready to strike out, at age nineteen—the summer before moving from California to the Pacific Northwest.

"I wanted queer visibility," she says. "I was also rejecting coolness and exaggerating a nerdy style, wearing huge Buddy Holly glasses, bowties, and hand-stenciled sharpied Ts that said things like 'I am not a beefcake, I am a cupcake.'"

In Portland, as our friendship sweetened, this cupcake slowly returned to embracing her queer femme heart. After just over a decade as Dexter, she decided to return to the name Rhiannon.

"I had literally started stuttering over introducing myself as Dexter," Rhiannon says. "It just didn't feel like my name anymore. This coincided with me getting further in touch with my witchy roots and upbringing, and I was creating altars and rituals more again. I had been given this beautiful, powerful name with the intention that it would help me on a life path of feeling strong, fiery, and capable, and I wondered what my life might be like with the name Rhiannon."

So it was with a nod to her matrilineage and a deep connection to Stevie Nicks, that Rhiannon reclaimed Rhiannon, the name her mother gave her, witch of transformation and retransformation.

As a singer, Rhiannon naturally turns to the witchy traditions of chanting and magical song to raise energy,

amplify ritual, and set loud intention to
slay the patriarchy.

She offers us the spell of
Rhiannon—no matter what our
mamas named us.

Listen to Fleetwood
Mac's song about the old
Welsh witch, "Rhiannon,"
before you begin this
one—and remember
to rule your life like
a bird in flight.

Take It Back Spell

RHIANNON FLOWERS

I was named after the powerful fairy goddess shape shifter Rhiannon, known for her compassion and her wrath.

"I gave you this name because I wanted you to have deep compassion for people but not to take any shit from anyone," my mom told me when I was a kid. My name itself is a spell cast for me by my high-priestess mother.

I didn't know until I was a teenager with a thrifted cassette tape that my mom had us all singing the Tears for Fears song "Shout" in pagan rituals she led when I was a child. We shouted, we let it all out, each taking turns wailing into the circle the things we could do without. "Racism! Patriarchy! Abuse! Fatphobia! The rape of Mother Earth!"

"Self-doubt!" I yelled from the depths of my twelve-year-old tummy.

The truth is, I often struggle to feel in my power. In my band Whisper Hiss, when I sing is when I feel most in touch with my inner strength. In one of my songs I simply repeat: "Take your power back!"

In this, we call our power back to us from all the places it has been taken from us unwillingly and where we've given it away. We reclaim our power from the patriarchy, toxic relationships, jobs, past experiences, and old belief systems so that we may fully embody ourselves.

You are the safe container for all of your brilliance, anger, and every feeling that is brewing in the cauldron of your being. This is a spell to reinforce that truth.

Begin

1. Say aloud: *Rhiannon, witch of transformation, sing your wisdom to me as I embrace the strengths of vulnerability. Bring self-compassion as I invite my wrath to the table. I call on you to help me fully inhabit my body, with a brewing of butterflies sung out of my mouth, moonstones and amethysts drawn to my chest in protection, I awaken myself. I call my power back to me!*

2. Visualizing all the places and moments your power was taken or given from you, chant: *I take my power back!*

3. May the frequency of our combined voices be too loud for the patriarchy to withstand! Compassionately witness yourself coming into your strength. Chant: *By the power of three by three, as I will it so shall it be.*

Take your power back!
Do no harm, but take no shit.
Blessed be.

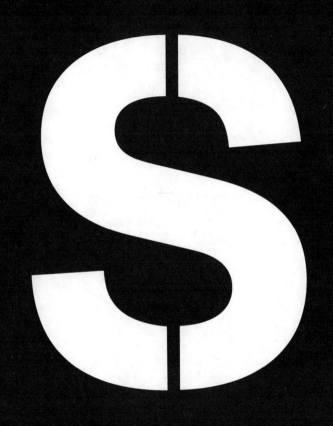

SOCIAL JUSTICE

The shape of the
letter ∫ originates
in the curve of
the archer's bow.
Take aim.

Make Cool Designs And Send Them Into Congress To Do Your Bidding

When I went to Iceland in June, the sun never set. There was supposed to be a queer nightclub around the corner from the basement apartment where I was staying, but the nightclub never opened. So instead I climbed into a blue rental car and drove up toward the Arctic Circle.

I tried to imagine living someplace so cold where I was related to pretty much everyone, where sometimes the sun didn't set for months, and when it did it didn't come up again for a long time.

I like herring. And rye bread. The diet wouldn't be a problem for me. But I think I would need some serious magic.

Three hours north of Reykjavik, in the port town of Hólmavik, I pulled into the dirt and gravel driveway of the Museum of Icelandic Sorcery & Witchcraft.

In old-school Iceland, where the witches were the poorest people, popular magical tools included a protective carving called the Helm of Awe, dolls that helped steal milk, and an intricate process for achieving invisibility. Most of the spells include staves—or standardized sigils—which are basically cool secret symbols that witches use to get what they need.

Making and using sigils is so easy and effective, many witches end up relying on them as their primary—or sole—manifestation technique.

What's not to like: we make cool symbols to represent our intentions. We charge them and release them. And then our intentions are out there battling the patriarchy even as we sleep.

Try this:

Symbolism for the Win

1. Write down the name of a feminist powerhouse you'd like to see elected and add the words "has taken office" or "wins reelection" or "is president of the United States"—or some other phrasing to suggest the win has already happened and her opponent has conceded:

2. .... is president of the United States

3. Remove all the vowels, and remove all the repeating letters, so you're left with a string of consonants, perhaps something like this:

lxndrcstzph

5. Combine the letters into a design. Paint the design onto a rock with water, and let it evaporate in the sun. In this way, your intention has been absorbed into the atmosphere.

Related to the practice of making spells from sigils, by concentrating our intentions into simplified letter-based symbols, is the practice of creating servitors.

I propose that today—whenever this spell finds you—we each create a servitor for social justice. These are just going to be little magical beings that we can psychically send into all the courthouses of the world to whisper into all the judges' ears: Black lives matter, trans rights are human rights, women have sovereignty over their own bodies, no person is illegal, do your job and protect the vulnerable.

I asked Iowa midwife Melanie Hexen, famous for binding notorious predators and a-holes, to school us on both.

Sigils and Servitors for Social Justice

FROM MELANIE HEXEN

Create a Sigil

A sigil can be for your name, to represent someone, or used for a full-on spell. It's simply a symbol used to represent something. This process can be used for social justice or personal development. You can burn a sigil to help end gun violence, or carry a sigil to help you speak your mind.

Gather

Writing supplies

1 blue candle

Begin

1. Write out your specific message for your sigil. For instance, "I want social justice for women who are victims of rape."

2. Drop all the unnecessary words, drop the vowels, and drop repeat letters, so it looks like this:

scljtcwmnvrp

3. Take those letters and make a cool design. Don't get too hung up on artistic ability. You got this.

4. Scratch that sigil into a blue candle and burn it for three days. On the fourth day, toss the whole thing into a fire or plant it in a garden. Or whatever imitates the intention.

Create a Servitor

A servitor is a little different from a sigil.
It's a magical *being* you create. You can believe
it's a real entity, or you can believe
it's a psychological exercise. Either way, it will work.

Here is how to make yours:

Gather

Art supplies (paper, pencil, clay)

Begin

1. Imagine this magical being in great detail. Mine are often small, but yours can be big. Draw a picture. Make a clay model. Vividly imagine everything. Clothes. Hair color. Voice. It doesn't need to be human although mine usually are. You can give it attributes to help with a particular task—maybe big teeth, or octopus arms, or superpower hearing.

2. Name your servitor if you like.

3. When you need a job done, summon your servitor. Do this by calling its name or drawing its sigil or just imagining it present.

4. Command your servitor to do your bidding. Give it a clear task: *Turn off the lights I left on. Guard my house. Support my friend Diane in divorce court. Torment the Klansman at the end of the street. Go to the judges in the county courthouse and whisper in their ears.*

You can use the same servitor over and over. If you wish, you can reward its good deeds with treats like whiskey or milk or chocolate or even blood—but its best reward is your attention.

You can have a lifelong relationship with this being, or it can be a one-job deal. I have found that the more I do this, the more powerful my servitors become. It can be the same for you. Don't underestimate yourself as a witch. You're strong and powerful.

And the thing is, you can't do it wrong. The words are yours and, if spoken with truth and passion, will work. The power is yours. If something in witchcraft ever scares you, just tell it to go the fuck away. You are a powerful witch. The more you practice witchcraft, the stronger you'll become. That's why it's called practicing.

TRUST TREES

The runic *T*, which takes its name from Tyr, the one-handed Norse god of common justice, asks us to meditate on this: "What is higher than the self is the Self Becoming Higher." In other words, climb a tree.

When Human Culture Wears You Down, Get Woodsy With Your Nonhuman Allies

Witches and trees share a long and storied past. In places with forests, that's where we met—under the walnut or the holly branches. We felt a sense of secrecy and a safety under the cover of trees, but we also drew strength from their alliance. Many of us—as the outsiders in patriarchal communities—lived on the edges of town, in the forests.

If as a kid you felt a kinship with trees, I think that's one sign you were born to be a witch. Can you see any trees from where you are now? Send them a psychic greeting.

Summers and winters at my grandparents' place on Carmel Beach, I climbed my Monterey cypress. I knew every twist. Each year back, I'd start out gently, learning which branches could still hold me.

At my stepdad's house in California where I lived during the school years, I climbed the Australian tea tree in the side yard and sat under the oak tree out back when I wanted to talk with my owl.

I fantasize about living in a tree house with wings and roots and chicken legs. When I build it, I hope you'll come and visit.

I keep becoming a different person, but I always seem to have this same twist in my spine.

I dreamed my old buddy Moe Bowstern was a giant apple tree. I sent her a message in a bucket tied to a string: *Will you write a spell for us, Apple Tree who is Moe?*

She sent down three.

Apple trees are generous like that.

The more human part of Moe grew up in one of those assimilationist Catholic families that still believed in ghosts and hunches and accepted that sometimes you didn't have to use the phone to find out where people were. This was on the Seneca land of the Haudenosaunee. Swimming in the cold and beautiful lakes of that land helped Moe stay on the planet.

I met her out West, in Portland, when she was first experimenting with her magical powers. Now she's an initiate, honoring and retaining the magical lineage of Celtic and northern mysteries and working hard to heal her ancestral lines to address the violence, scarcity, abuse, alcoholism, and cancer she inherited. Her zine, *When a Witch . . .* , chronicles what she's learned.

Here are the three spells she offered us:

Tree Spells

MOE BOWSTERN

Trees are trustworthy allies. They support both vertical and horizontal communication lines. They hold each other up and keep each other alive. You can always trust a tree.

Trees are nourished by what we energetically shed, much as they are by our respiratory exhalations. I take my sorrow and my joy to my tree friends. I ask them to help me carry my burdens and take my fear and other things that don't serve me. The upper branches of the tree can brush my house clean. The roots can extract unhelpful, sinking energies that bog me down. In exchange, I notice my trees: I water them in the dry times. I pick their fruits and prune them. I give them my breath and attention. You can too.

Outdoor Tree Spell

Begin

1. Stand under a tree.

2. Take a big breath in. Close your eyes if it helps. Breath out. Do this a few times. With each breath in, expand yourself as a tree expands. With each breath out, push your breath down lower and lower in your body—chest, stomach, crotch, knees.

3. When you're ready, take in a big breath and exhale down through your feet and below your feet. Send your breath into the roots of the trees.

4. Put your hands on the tree. Breathe in. When you breathe, feel the tree giving you breath as it exhales oxygen. Breathe out into the roots and the mycelium. Feel the tree taking in your exhalations.

5. Try it the other way, breathing in from the roots, breathing in the nourishing darkness, and breathing out through your palms. Feel your connection to this tree. Through the mycelial network in the soil, feel your connection to all trees.

Trees as Home Protection Spell

Begin

1. Notice the trees around your home. If possible, perform the outdoor tree spell with one of the trees. This tree does not have to be on your "property," but must be visible or otherwise influence your home. Can you smell it? Do its roots ruck up your sidewalk?

2. If it feels right in your body, ask the tree to protect your home. Ask the tree to take up unhelpful energies cast off in the course of a day.

3. Thank the tree. Give it water, love, dreams. Fruit trees like it when you bury bones around.

Indoor Tree Spell

Is your house made of wood? Are there wood floors where you live or work? Shelving? Furniture? All began as trees.

Begin

1. Use your outdoor tree spell to find the tree inside the furniture or flooring. Remind the wood of its tree-ness; ask the wood about its tree-ness.

2. When you have connected to the tree-ness in the wood, remember that our ancient human ancestors used to live in trees. Notice that we still do. Using your connection to the tree-ness of the wood, with your breathing, connect to the trees of the outdoors with whom you have made relationships.

UNLEASHING
NEMESIS

The first recorded use of
U and *V* as distinct letters
is in a gothic alphabet from
1386. So put on your black
lipstick for this one.

Let the Goddess of Retribution And Reparations Explode In All Her Glorious Pent-Up Fury

U, like *N*, carries the energy of *the limit*. Where *N* says no and not in our names and never again. *U* undoes, unplugs, goes underground, uncoils, and finally unleashes. *U* reminds us that it's never too late to U turn and withdraw from a genocidal deal.

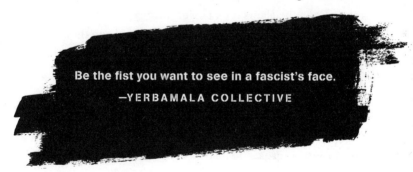

Be the fist you want to see in a fascist's face.
—YERBAMALA COLLECTIVE

And genocide, let's face it, is one of the patriarchy's specialties. Take Nazi Germany—one of the purest forms of patriarchy ever executed. Adolf Hitler, a guy who found it hard to relax around confident, outspoken, or professional women, brought his femme-phobia to government policy from the get-go. He thought pay equity for women was a communist plot. So one of the Nazis' first policy objectives was to get women out of the paid workforce and into the business of pumping out more Aryan babies. In 1933, the Nazi regime passed the Law for the Encouragement of Marriage and offered baby bonuses to white women.

Back in the 1920s, Germany had led the world developing contraceptives, including condoms, diaphragms, and IUDs. But the Nazis outlawed contraception—kind of like the GOP wants to do today—not only to increase the birthrate but because many pioneers of contraceptive medicine were Jewish.

Even *discussing* birth control was eventually banned.

It's sobering to think about how quickly everything can change. When the Nazis took power in 1933, there were some one hundred thousand female teachers and three thousand female doctors working in Germany. Under Hitler, they were forced to resign or pushed into marriage. Cabarets and jazz clubs were closed down in 1935. Local governments passed laws restricting women from singing, dancing, or appearing bare legged in public. The Nazis even commissioned fashion designers to create fascist dresses and get us out of our pants! Starting in 1936, women were prohibited from working as lawyers, judges, school principals, and in a bunch of other professions. University and college spots for women were restricted to a quota of 10 percent. The regime decried abortion as a "crime against the body and against the state"—but only for Aryan women. In 1938, a Nazi-run state court ruled that

abortion should be free and legal for all Jewish women despite the ban for non-Jews.

Pollster Kellyanne Conway horrifyingly echoed this kind of thinking in 2017 when she suggested that getting racist, white Americans to breed more is "how I think we fight these demographic wars moving forward."

Felicity Artemis, high priestess mother of Rhiannon Flowers and founder of the Artemis Institute for Radical Magick in Portland, is herself the daughter of Holocaust survivors.

She's all for clandestine spells when that's what the times call for, but she knows how to make public magic, too. She once got herself booked on a Sunday morning talk show on a big commercial radio station and proceeded to lead a meditation to decrucify Jesus! In this "Change or Die Hex," Felicity invokes Nemesis, the ancient Greek goddess of retribution and reparations whose name was derived from the Greek words meaning "dispenser of dues."

"As things heat up and the world is being hurled toward the dystopian wet dream of the patriarchy," Felicity says, "I feel ultimate urgency to make as much sense as possible, in as many ways as possible, as soon as possible." As such, she's at work on *The Art of the Hex: A Handbook of Radical Witchcraft.* "I'm all in," she says.

Are you?

As you contemplate this excellently rhyme-powered hex, notice what attachments to the system it brings up for you. (Like, *OMG, will my 401(k) suffer if the patriarchy falls?*)

As you read the hex, silently or aloud, identify some ways you can untie yourself, unplug, and uncoil—beginning today—from the systems you no longer wish to support. If you're a white or cis-male witch, ask yourself, *How can I begin to make reparations?*

Change or Die Hex

FELICITY ARTEMIS

Witches know that all intentions we send out in a spell will surely come back upon us exponentially—three times three times three. When we hex systems of injustice, we acknowledge our complicity, on various levels, in the systems of injustice and call upon our wisdom and power to accelerate our collective evolution to set things right.

Who

At least three participants.

Gather

Face paint (ash, charcoal, and red clay all work well)

Drums

Knives

1 overripe, wrinkled pomegranate

Your voices

Begin

Build a fire and form a circle around it.

Chant

And now, we give death to the system

■

As a sign that we be truly free
we who lay claim to witchery
come we naked to the rite
gather under veil of night.
Circle up now, far and wide,
to give ourselves this magick ride
the hell out of patriarchy.

■

It's time

■

to infiltrate the mind and heart
of the psychopath patriarch
that creates itself in every guise
to capture, rape, and colonize
and profit from Earth's demise
corralling us all to participate
in our own apocalyptic fate.
No time left to hesitate.

■

Let's kill it.

■

Faces painted—
ash and charcoal, blood red clay—
primal elemental way,
we call upon ancestral rage,
propel the spell and turn the page,
hurl us to our next stage evolution
becoming Nemesis, divine retribution,
we set things right, ignite revolution,
lighting the fire of enlightened solution.

■

Our victory is assured.

■

Wide-eyed humming, rise up drumming,
shape-shifters of our own becoming,
singing, screeching, in the biosphere's voice,
here at the crossroads of humanity's choice,
rattles shaking, Earth is quaking,
to bless this mythic undertaking.
We are the life force,
the power to change course,
to feel what is real to withdraw from the deal,
in delirious dance, raw emotion revealed.
Commune with the snake,
all senses awake in an altered state
now calling the furious Furies and Fates
the growl of the she-wolf protecting her young.
Baring our teeth
the spell has begun.

■

Let's do this.

■

Glistening knives to symbolize
our willful refusal to compromise.
Clink them together, together we rise
to the task.

■

Two of us carefully stab
each side of an old pomegranate, give it a jab.
Now raise it on high so we all can see
the heartless heart of patriarchy

that drives the whole machinery,
the system of atrocity.

■

Now watch it bleed…

■

All scream: *Die!*

■

The third person stabs the effigy:
This is for Judeo-Christianity,
the source of our insanity
the mythology of male supremacy,
all supremacist philosophies
that colonize,
dehumanize,
disguise the nature of reality.
No more this lie,
it's time to die!

■

Now throw the shitshow in the fire,
incanting as the flames grow higher:
Destroy the lie! Change or die!
Watch as the fire consumes it.

■

May this blaze uncraze and grace
the world with empathy
as the new ethos of all humanity.

■

As we will it, so shall it be.

■

VISUALIZATION

The letter *U* and the letter *V* were one and the same for millennia. Then *U* wanted to be a vowel, and *V* wanted to be a consonant, and they agreed to see different words.

Picture Mother Spider Nabbing The Patriarch Where He Lives

Ever wonder why the Nazis didn't get past the Channel Islands and invade Britain during World War II? Given the German war machine and the fact that Britain's National Socialist Party was kind of a major enemy of Hitler's genocidal capitalist fascism?

Historians of war have their explanations—and you can read about those in all the standard textbooks and narratives of war—but magical historians know that in 1939, immediately following Britain's declaration of war, the British high priestess Dion Fortune started writing regular letters to the members of her secret magical order, the Fraternity of the Inner Light, a tributary of the Order of the Golden Dawn. These magic makers were unable to meet in person because of wartime travel restrictions, so Dion organized the group's visualizations to invoke protection, keep up morale, and create an overall "psychic resistance."

Because of the genocidal emergency, the Fraternity of the Inner Light for the first time opened its doors to anyone who wanted to learn their methods of esoteric mind magic.

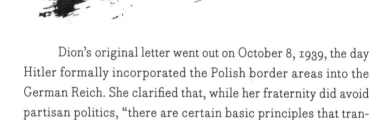

Nothing happens in the "real" world unless
it first happens in the images in our head.
—GLORIA E. ANZALDÚA,
Borderlands/La Frontera: The New Mestiza

Dion's original letter went out on October 8, 1939, the day
Hitler formally incorporated the Polish border areas into the
German Reich. She clarified that, while her fraternity did avoid
partisan politics, "there are certain basic principles that tran-
scend all partisanship"—namely, pushing back against fascism.

Nearly eight decades later, Erika Wanenmacher—Santa
Fe's famous Ditch Witch and unrepentant maker of magical
things who built part of *House of Eternal Return,* an installa-
tion by Meow Wolf, an arts and entertainment group based in
Santa Fe—was inspired by Dion's account of the anti-Nazi visualizations chronicled in *The Magical Battle of Britain.* Erika
invited the witches in her extended circle to start doing some
pro-active magic. Together, they would visualize a mother spider to help us out of this patriarchal mess. Spiders are nature's

great weavers—they gently and powerfully ensnare their prey in their webs—and have long been associated with feminine power. Their eight legs suggest the symbol of infinity, so Mother Spider is the infinite Mama Goddess backup.

One of the things that impressed Erika about Dion's circle was that they only worked with positive, protective aspects—no naming of names, no banishing, no targeting of individuals. It's not the only way to go about hexing, but it's valid and has some good history.

Mother Spider Visualization

ERIKA WANENMACHER

Begin

1. Sit. Close your eyes. Ground. Breathe. Call your corners.

2. Visualize a protective circle of golden sparkles around yourself, spiraling out through your room, your neighborhood, your town, the deserts, the forests, the fields, the mountains, the waters. As the sparkles move, the creatures take notice and lift their heads—rats, raccoons, horses, hawks, whales, coyotes, mice, bees, ants. Something's happening. They're listening. See your circle spiral out into space, surrounding Earth and her blanket of clouds with the sparkling golden circle of protection.

3. Visualize yourself standing shoulder to shoulder in a rowdy crowd around the White House. It's night, but the area is brightly lit. There are chants and signs and cheers—optimistic, not angry. The crowd hushes because the mother of all spiders drops down from the sky onto the top of the White House! She has made a giant web, and we're holding onto the web structure. She sits right down on the White House, and as the patriarch comes running out, Mother Spider scoops him up and winds him in a ball of her silk and the crowd *cheers!*

4. Then she captures his cronies and does it again, over and over, binding and rolling them and hanging them in the web, saving them for later. We're holding onto the web, and we can feel the vibrations of the captures, wriggling and trying to escape. Mother Spider does a little vaudeville-like tap dance, takes a bow, and gathers up the bound patriarch and his crony bundles and flings them up into the darkness, then climbs up her thread after them.

5. All eyes follow her until she disappears. We turn and look at each other, ecstatic, introducing ourselves, chatting, familiar, and realize that we have been holding hands, humans and creatures alike. Hand in paw, claw in flipper, fin in leaves, roots in teeth. *We are the web! We are the structure! Power to the planet!*

6. As you come back to your body, sit for a few minutes more with your eyes closed. Feel the power circling through you, sparkling. Breathe. We can do this.

7. Open your eyes.

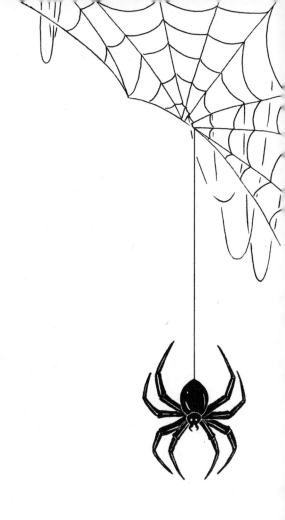

WALLET CHARM

The only letter whose name gives no clue as to its pronunciation, *W* was kind of the breakup child of *U* and *V*. And thank the Goddess. Because who wants to be called a vitch?

Make a Protective Amulet and Carry It With You To Ward Off Bigotry

———

Our taxi weaves in and out of traffic and alleys, avoiding the quicker toll roads, and finally spits us out on Nak Niwat, a puddled street in northeast Bangkok.

Here, between Yes! Dentist and Pun-Pun Pet Salon, is Bangkok's famous pagan meeting spot, Ace of Cups: The Witch Café.

Inside, books and crystals line exposed-brick walls. A group of students huddle around a small table discussing the tarot. Post-it Notes with runes and staves decorate a bulletin board like reminders. Behind the counter and a sign that warns, "A witch lives here with her little monsters," Atiwan Kongsorn makes potions, cappuccino, and cake. A chalkboard next to the cash register lists zodiac sodas.

Aries: Lychee watermelon
Taurus: Green apple kiwi
Gemini: Pomegranate peach
Cancer: Strawberry raspberry

Leo: Mango peach
Virgo: Lychee rose
Libra: Coconut banana
Scorpio: Black currant pomegranate
Sagittarius: Rose passionflower
Capricorn: Banana caramel
Aquarius: Double mint
Pisces: Mint Curacao

We order the Cancerian for myself, the Virgo for Maxito, and the Aries for my biological father, who we're in Thailand to visit. We'll share a witch brownie.

Atiwan gets to work, conjuring it all up.

I've heard Atiwan say that magic making is like cooking: everyone can do it, but some people can do it better than others. Practice helps, as does knowing your ingredients and, when possible, sourcing them locally.

He comes from a long line of Eastern witches who know the power of protective

amulets carried on the body. When he added Western witch-craft to his repertoire, he saw that Bangkok needed a space for its Wiccan community to gather, so he and his partner manifested The Witch Café. Not instantly—it took seven years and some serious sweat—but magic rewards the hard worker.

When I wrote to Atiwan from home, asking if he could concoct a spell against patriarchy and racism, he said, "Count me in. I'm seeing a wallet charm."

The idea of carrying charms for luck and protection is ancient and cross-cultural. When witches passed each other in the woods in England, they sometimes handed each other acorns to signal "Team Witch!"—and the acorns themselves served to protect against illness. When I was pregnant in Italy, all the old women advised me to carry a little *cornicello* horn to ward off the evil eye. In Ghana and the African diaspora, practitioners carry *gris-gris* bags to stop gossip and ward off bullshit.

Atiwan's wallet charm against the patriarchy uses *Angelica;* varieties of this genus grow all over temperate and subarctic regions of the Northern Hemisphere. Called wild angelica, garden angelica, root of the Holy Ghost, *dong quai,* or *bai zhi,* these related species tend to sprout up near riverbanks, and all are known for their magical qualities of protection.

He walked me through making the charm.

Empowered Angelica Wallet Charm

ATIWAN KONGSORN

When

Best performed on a Saturday.

Gather

1 slice of dried angelica root*

Dragon's blood ink**

Frankincense, sage, or salt

1 candle or incense

* You should be able to get dried angelica root at an herb store or online. If you have a local Chinese medicinal store, choose the *dong quai* or *bai zhi*—the bai zhi is a little cheaper and will work well. Select or break off a piece of the root slice that's big enough to write on but small enough to fit in your wallet.

** Dragon's blood ink is available at most spiritual supply stores. If you don't have access to dragon's blood, you may improvise and use another red ink.

Begin

1. As with any spell, you may light a candle, burn some incense, or smudge for cleansing. I use frankincense for smudging; sage would have to be imported from the United States. But if you have sage available locally, it will certainly do. Any method of cleansing will do as well—even salt and water. Mentally preparing is the top priority, so we use the ingredients that are accessible and we use our focused minds.

2. For the protection spell, you want your thoughts to be strong but not too aggressive. You're ready to fight, but you don't want to provoke the enemy. Ground yourself by visualizing roots from your body into the earth, like the angelica root itself.

3. Call the elements and your personal deity. Focus on what you want to be protected from—racism and misogyny or more specific enemies—and with the dragon's blood, write the rune Algiz with seven extra strokes on the right side. It's a code to double Algiz, which is a rune for protection, and so it becomes protection with protection. (The rune Algiz looks like an upside-down peace sign without the circle around it or a man with arms upraised. Draw this three-pronged Y and then add seven extra strokes or prongs on the right side.)

4. You may empower the charm with one or more additional protective helpers, such as a sprinkle of black salt or mugwort, the smoke of sage or *palo santo* (*Bursera graveolens*), or a drop of anointing oil. Focus on who and what you want to protect.

5. When you're finished, thank your deity, thank the elements, and close your ritual in a way that's meaningful to you.

Keep your charm in your wallet so that you always have it close. And be careful out there. Things can change quickly. You're strong, not too aggressive, protected.

XOANON

One of the least-used letters of our alphabet, X knows that other letters can make the same sound: the two C'S of SUCCESS, say, or the CKS of ducks. But X knows she's indispensable. X marks the spot. X casts the ballot. X is the unknown we solve for. X promises it's going to be sexy—or at least top secret. X is the signature of Marie Laveau. X is Malcolm, too. X seals it with a consensual kiss.

Carve A Feminist Icon Out Of Wood And Listen To What She Says

———

When my stepdad's father was out of work in the early 1930s, he'd take the train from Palo Alto to San Francisco every day to see what he could find. On the way, he carved seahorses out of soft wood. Bronze castings of his seahorses decorated the Steinhart Aquarium in San Francisco for decades. Male seahorses are cool in that they take on the pregnancies in the community: they're the ones who carry the female's eggs in a tail pouch for their month-and-a-half gestation.

When my stepfather's father carved those seahorses, I wonder what the seahorses told him.

Seahorse spirit says: *When everyone takes part in nurturing new life, we'll all be less likely to be so cavalier about abuse.*

Seahorse spirit says: *There's no need to throw the entire male gender out with the patriarchy's bathwater.*

Seahorse spirit says: *Be an artist, not a Nazi.*

Hand-whittling a xoanon—or a little wooden effigy— is an old-school way to let a spirit show you its form. We find xoanons and evidence of xoanons in ancient Greece, and they're kind of like little pocket goddesses—often of Artemis, the queer midwife deity. We know xoanons were considered powerful,

because "idolatry" became one of the things Judeo-Christian patriarchs really got their panties in a wad about.

Unlike when we make a poppet, where we're fashioning a doll into human form with the intention of influencing change in the seen world, we carve a xoanon to give shape to unseen deities or muses with the intention of letting them guide and protect us. Basically, it's a portable goddess to have at our side. Your xoanon might even speak to you. Christianity taught many of us not to listen to voices for fear of the devil's voice, but what's the devil?

Maybe the devil is the false belief that we need our oppressors in order to stay alive.

If you hear voices instructing you to harm yourself or anyone else, or to otherwise identify with your oppressors, tell them "no fucking way." Witches don't give the time of day to *every* voice we hear—just the ones that sound compassionate and sane.

I asked my sister Leslie Selene, a spiritual medium and author of *Inviting Her In: Diary of a Witch,* to carve a xoanon for us and show us how it's done.

Reacquaintance with Idolatry

LESLIE SELENE

I choose a piece of driftwood that's been lying on my altar for a few years. A field guide picked it up on the trail when we were hiking at the fairy bridge, near the springs at Rennes-les-Bains in Southern France. He handed it to me, said, "There's a spirit inside the wood that wants to talk to you." So I've been saving it.

The first thing to emerge is her crown. On her brow, a crescent moon lies on its side, to hold a blooming rose. Large horns arch gently from behind each ear, to frame her delicate features.

Scraping away the pulp alongside her nose and across the cheekbones, her smooth face is revealed. A tear falls from her eye and stains a thin cobalt line down to her chin.

My Opinel picnic knife is sharp enough, and I whittle away the dregs of the forest floor that are stuck to her sides. I find my driftwood is half blond, half cerulean. Her form stretches out, pushing against the blade to define itself.

Tentatively, she touches the hem of her cape. Her skirt tapers inward. At first I wonder where she puts her feet, but then I see it. From the breast down, she's a snake, or a horse, or a bird.

I begin to suspect it might be her, when the tip refuses to become a fin, or be refined to a point. At the bottom is the head of a snake, not the tail.

This means she has two heads, and also that she has two genders, which makes her very old, indeed. I recognize her at last—Xamaràn or Sahmaran, deva of love and fertility, sacred in Kurdish traditions.

I smooth the splinters from her eyes and the dust from between her scales, but I leave her rough hewn. I won't polish away her wildness. When I've rubbed her porous skin with oil, darkened her horns with ash, waxed her teal cloak, and dabbed perfume on the flowers in her crown, I ask her to speak.

She doesn't speak in words, or if she does, it's the language of birdsong. My bones resonate with the sound. When my cells translate the vibrations to my ears, it comes out as a hiss: "Sister! Your comrades are being murdered in cold blood. Anarchist freedom fighters and ecofeminists just like you are laying down their lives as we speak, defending the rights of women, of rivers, and of trees. Unite. We are now too many to hold back!"

Try whittling your own xoanon. See what she says.

Gather

A piece of driftwood

1 candle

Whittling knife

Oil

Ash

Wax

Perfume

Begin

1. Light your candle. Watch your wood in the flickering light to see if she changes. Maybe the shadows will show you her face.

2. Pick up the wood and turn her over in your hands to get a closer look. Maybe her bark is rough in places, and spongy in other spots. Begin to clean her up. Underneath that first layer, her skin will be smooth.

3. Smooth any splinters from your xoanon's eyes and any dust from between her limbs but leave her rough hewn. Don't polish away her wildness.

4. Now, use your oil and ash and wax and perfume to anoint your xoanon. Rub her porous skin with oil, perhaps darken her horns with ash, wax her cloak, and dab perfume on her crown.

5. Ask her to speak. Ask her to defend the rights of women, of rivers, and of trees.

YEMAYÁ

Y is the hybrid bisexual
of the alphabet, at once
a vowel and a consonant.
The runic *Y* defends
all that we love.

TAP INTO THE DIVINE FEMININE FOR BOTH HER GENTLE LOVE AND HER SIREN-WRATH-POWER TO LURE VILE PEOPLE TO THEIR DEATHS

The mermaid emerges from the waves, and asks, "Don't people know the ocean is sacred?"

The people say, *Yes, of course.*

She asks: "Then what's up with the 'great Pacific garbage patch' that's three times the size of France floating out there between Hawaii and California? Seriously? Mama goes on *one* well-deserved self-care retreat, and this is what she comes back to? Eighty thousand tons of plastic?"

The pollutants in the garbage patch range in size from abandoned fishing nets to the micropellets used in our abrasive cleansers. And here's the payback: not all of what ends up in the great garbage patch stays in the great garbage patch. Fish and sea turtles eat the plastic. Fish eat other fish. Plastic-fed fish become our ceviche. Everything that comes from the sea now has a measurable amount of plastic in it.

This is hardly the way to act as a gracious guest on this bountiful planet.

I decided to go out to San Diego to consult with the ocean about this. Her salty waters felt like home. I'd spent a lot of summers as a kid visiting my Gammie Evelyn here, and all I ever wanted to do was play in the surf and get pummeled and ride the waves and come up gasping, exhilarated.

I'd run up the beach, exhausted, to where my Gammie Evelyn read her *Vogue* magazine or *W* in her lounge chair. She'd set down her magazine and open the wicker picnic basket she'd packed with Fresca and tuna fish sandwiches.

I understood the epitome of the difference between my Gammie Evelyn and me in these moments: I watched, in awe of the fact that she never got sand in her sandwich as she ate. I felt messy, but I still felt loved.

Now my Gammie Evelyn was ten years dead, but my old partner in witch crime Inga Aaron—mother, divine feminine propagator, and priestess of Yemayá—lived near San Diego. So I got an early flight.

I asked Inga if she thought it was too presumptuous for noninitiates to petition Yemayá for help in toppling the patriarchy. Yemayá, the mermaid deity of the Yoruba religion and the mother of all the orishas, is often syncretized with Our Lady of Regla in the Afro-Cuban diaspora. Her ritual salutation is "Omío Yemayá."

Inga smiled generous the way she does and said, "Yemayá welcomes all her children."

She'll welcome you, too. Call her and she will come.

Petition Yemayá

INGA AARON

When

Best performed on a night with a crescent moon.

Where

Close proximity to a body of water.
The ocean is wonderful, but any natural body
of water is OK. She will hear us.

Who

Seven participants, or any multiple of seven.

Gather

1 large, shallow basket

1 large piece of blue, sturdy fabric

Molasses

7 dimes per participant

White flower petals

Begin

1. We begin by acknowledging that Yemayá is not happy with the ways the patriarchy is killing Earth and all her inhabitants. Throughout the African diaspora, Yemayá is revered for her gentle love as well as the ferocity of her wrath. Right now, in a tumultuous and violent world that seeks to sink deeper into oppression and malignant misogyny, we must circle and fight back.

2. As the divine feminine rises to eliminate the patriarchy, we may petition Yemayá to assist us in the process.

3. We, in her image, are also very powerful, particularly in circle and in ritual. Let us invoke the nurturing and ferocious energy of Yemayá.

∎

On a night with a crescent moon, dress in shades of blue. Place a large blue cloth inside a large basket. Place a watermelon in the basket. Place other spell ingredients on the ground near the basket.

∎

Begin to walk around the basket in a circle. Each participant may call out their prayer, their desire, their fear, and their incantation as they stop and pour some molasses over the watermelon, shred white flowers and sprinkle them over the molasses, and then place seven dimes on top. The circle keeps moving until every petitioner has spoken.

■

This circle will become highly energetic and intense. These are dire times. Speak out loud while you are circling. Call out the perpetrators of patriarchal harm. Call them out by name. Call out the government that seeks to silence us. Call out those who have used their gender to harm the planet. Sing, pray, undulate, incant, visualize, manifest, believe.

The circle will feel when it's time to fold its power into the blanket by gathering the edges and tying them around all of the ingredients of our petition into a bundle.

Now take the bundle, heavy with fruit, treats, hope, joy, anger, and sadness, to the water and leave it for Yemayá in a trashcan nearby.

Leave it *all* there.

It has been spoken.

Omío Yemayá.

ZODIAC

The last and least-used
letter of our alphabet,
Z is associated with the
tarot's magician, drawing
power down from the
spiritual world above
to the material world
below via his Z-shaped
lightning bolt. Like, ZAP!

Take Your Cues From The Stars And Volunteer For Campaigns To Elect Anticapitalist Women Of Color

―――

I'm sitting in the back of The Future in the Witch District in Minneapolis, casually chatting with a few ghosts who've been keeping me company during my magical creative residency. One old hag who doesn't like to tell anyone her name takes a puff of her menthol cigarette and laughs. "Why's everybody so afraid of death?" She grabs a handful of tortilla chips. "Tell 'em at least you can still smoke over here." She kind of cackles, and when she does, I recognize her as my old witchy elder from Sonoma County. "Z," she announces suddenly, "is for zodiac."

She gestures to the ceiling, which instantly becomes the sky, and she starts reciting assignments for the revolution, like horoscopes:

> *Aries: Protect children and elders.*
> *Taurus: Volunteer for campaigns to elect anticapitalist women of color.*
> *Gemini: Take over the media. Smash the binary gender system. Be bisexual.*

Cancer: Feed the revolutionaries as you become regally comfortable in your own authority.

Leo: Dress up like a queen and make street theater.

Virgo: Draft plans for specific aspects of moral liberation such as alternatives to money.

Libra: Serve as an ambassador of friendly flirtation and mutual understanding.

Scorpio: Engage in hot sex magic and keep your spy secrets.

Sagittarius: Travel if they'll give you a passport. Confront exploitation.

Capricorn: Plant a garden and work toward specific ecorevolutionary goals.

Aquarius: Quietly rebel against everything and make bold, public street art.

Pisces: Set up creative and sustainable systems for reparations.

As soon as I've jotted down the hag's proclamations, a bell rings and a man walks into the shop. The sky becomes ceiling again as the ghosts drift away, gossiping among themselves.

The man smiles wide. "I'm Zyon. I'm here to teach the astrology class."

"And maybe you have a zodiac spell for me against the patriarchy?" I ask.

Zyon nods like a man who is accustomed to such requests. He says, "Yes, and I have a feeling my colleague My Fourwinds can help with us with that."

A few weeks later, when I'm back home, their missive arrives in the mail.

Twelve Ways to Freedom Spell

ZYON GRAY AND MY FOURWINDS

We intend this to be a transformative spell and used the Hawai'ian forgiveness practice Ho'oponopono concept of healing. Four parts intention (earth, air, fire, water) plus three parts revolution (cardinal, fixed, mutable) equals twelve ways to freedom.

Gather

4 white chime candles

1 fire-safe container large enough to hold the four candles

Rocks—enough to cover the bottom of container and keep the candles fixed in place

Begin

1. Speak aloud as you light a candle for each element:

   Aries fire, spark of desire, calling my will into action.

   Taurus earth, solid molecules of matter, pressed by weight of gravity into vessel form.

2. Breathe the sound of ancestral memory drumming as you say:

   Gemini air, I release all habits of mind and thought that cause me to label that which is inside and outside myself.

3. Envision channels carrying knowledge and feeling to all parts of your body as you say:

   Cancer, water, I say to myself in all shades and corners of our Earth, our home, I love you.

4. Say these words as you meditate on the candle for each element:

   Leo, fire, burn away fear to reveal and embrace my true self, the core of my gift and purpose for coming here, to this time and place.

   I say to myself and anyone I have hurt or wronged, I am sorry.

   Virgo, earth, shining minerals of rock, each as varied, unique, and perfect as the faces of the peoples we are, natural and equal.

   I say to myself and any others wearing scars, forgive me.

   Libra, air, tribes meet with a smile and handshake, allies chant together a unifying vision of our relatedness.

Scorpio, water, deep stillness of mystery, well of emotion, compels me by magnetic forces toward connection with the divine.

5. Say these words as you extinguish the candle for each element:

■

Sagittarius, fire, embers spread interchange of cultural teachings from distant regions enriching our known ways.

Capricorn, earth, forms monuments to a new and fair society built with deliberation by hands of all nations.

Aquarius, air, breeze holding kite flying high above, marking learned lessons from past mistakes, brings wisdom from within.

I say, in gratitude, for consideration, kindness and respect, thank you.

Pisces, water, ocean's tide pulls at our shadow, our hidden motives, our unremembered dreams, with longing for submerging one into the whole.

I say, in speaking this elemental zodiac, bring light, energy, and healing into my cells, my vessel, my body, as a representative cell in the larger organism that is our living Earth, for a transformative remodeling of our human life.

It is so.

BE YOUR OWN MUSE

t makes me happy that Britain's first blue plaque historical marker for a witch was also its first blue plaque on a public housing project. I mean, *I* always pictured Doreen Valiente, that codebreaker against the Nazis who also wrote "The Charge of the Goddess," turning patriarchs into frogs from some crooked cottage in the woods—but it turns out her home was a postwar high-rise of council flats.

We don't have to be aristocracy to change the fucking world.

When my daughter, Maia, and I make the pilgrimage to Brighton some twenty-seven years after my initiation, an old woman with pink hair is crouched down in front of the plaque smoking a cigarette. The smoke rises up like an offering: "Doreen Valiente: Poet, Author, & Mother of Modern Witchcraft Lived Here."

We're in England to claim Maia's British citizenship—a status that the government here has finally decided was denied to her unfairly at birth due to the ridiculous notion of "illegitimacy."

Laws can change—sometimes for the equitable.

Back in London the next day, my friend Gossia gives me a pink pin from the Frida Kahlo exhibition that says *I am my own muse.*

At the Atlantis Bookshop, the occult hub run by mother-and-daughter team Geraldine and Bali Beskin, they've got the new David Bowie–themed tarot deck.

The Beskins love books, of course, and Bali wants to know when mine is coming out, but they're third- and fourth-generation practitioners, as well, so they're all about practice. Geraldine's advice to witches is down to earth: "Stay in one evening a week and get better at something. It may be embarrassing when you first try and call the quarters with only the cat for company, but you cannot drive a car by just reading *The Highway Code*."

Wherever I go, everyone I meet tells me someplace new I must go to gather even more energy to hex the patriarchy. They, too, have been focusing and practicing.

In a quiet pub near Angel, I meet up with Fiona Lensvelt, a former obituary writer and book reviewer for the *London Times* who coruns Litwitchure, London's only literary tarot cabaret and consultancy. She and her partner trained with Suzanne Corbie at the famous Treadwell's Bookstore, and they now read tarot cards for writers and other bookish types. She wears a gauzy black dress and bright red lipstick and asks what first drew me to witchcraft.

I say, "Witches have agency."

Fiona grew up Irish and Catholic, so she likes the story about my stepdad's excommunication from the church and subsequent magic making. When the hierophant appears in my reading, she decides it represents my stepfather's reinvention of the church: spiritual power without the structural weapons of privilege.

We pull more cards from the Rider-Waite-Smith deck. The fool crowns the spread.

"Inspirational," Fiona says.

Our prospects for hexing the patriarchy look bright.

The future is magical; the work is practical. We clarify our intentions and make our plans. We take action with stealth and adaptability. We cast spells in part to keep the wind at our backs.

Fiona points to the nine of pentacles. "Ah," she says, "this is the card we like to call Cher! You know, there's this great quote that Cher gave in an interview once. Her mother said, 'Sweetheart, settle down and marry a rich man,' and Cher said, 'Mom, I *am* a rich man.'"

I show Fiona the pin from Gossia, and she says, "Absolutely!" So we psychically pin it on tarot Cher's fancy cloak.

I understand the arc of my tarot reading to say: *We are our own muses. And the whole patriarchal, white supremacist, capitalist war machine is gonna be, like, Ribbit.*

ACKNOWLEDGMENTS

Thank you to my superstar editor, Laura Mazer, who helped shape this book from the start. Thanks to Chin-Yee Lai and Shreya Gupta for bringing their own supernatural visions to the project. Thanks to Kate Mueller, Brynn Warriner, and the production team at Seal Press for ironing out the details.

Thanks to all the contributors who went above and beyond, channeling and experimenting to hone their hexes for this political emergency that is late-stage capitalist patriarchy.

Thanks to Moe Bowstern, who has edited most of my books, for stepping in when I panicked with this one. It's good to have a co-conspirator adept in both word and magic. Thanks also to Adrian Shirk, Rhea Wolf, and Neesha Powell-Twagirumukiza for lending your brilliance and discernment to early drafts.

Thanks to Lacey Prpić Hedtke and The Future in Minneapolis for granting me the creative residency where I began to compile these spells.

Thanks to Joe Zirker, my favorite white man and dissident art star. It's like they say in that Freakwater song, "There's nothing so pure as the kindness of an atheist."

Thanks to Jeremy Adam Smith and China Martens for their help testing the hex anthems.

Thanks to the Morris Pratt Institute for the correspondence courses on modern Spiritualism.

Thanks to my family—Deena Chafetz, Maia Swift, and Maximilian Gore-Perez—for being good-humored carry-on-only traveling companions as we circled the globe looking for the best hexes.

Thanks to Aïsha Kent, our amazing witch-tour guide in London—you are magic! Not to mention subversively funny. And thanks to Saskia Kent for your friendship all these years.

Thanks to all the magical writers in The Literary Kitchen. You inspire me.

Thanks, always, to my kickass writing group: Karin Spirn, Michelle Cruz Gonzales, and Tomas Moniz. You are the very best.

Thank you to the spirits and the ancestors.

And thanks to all the other witches against the patriarchy, known and unknown to me—I feel your power increasing exponentially and daily.

Sending love and power from here!

—Ariel Gore

INDEX OF WITCHERY

ABOUT THE AUTHOR

Ariel Gore is an award-winning editor, journalist, and the author of a dozen previous books of fiction and nonfiction including the novel *We Were Witches*. The founding editor of *Hip Mama,* her articles and essays have also appeared in *Psychology Today, Salon, The San Francisco Chronicle, The Rumpus,* and elsewhere. She's currently manifesting the matriarchy in Santa Fe, New Mexico, where she lives.

SEAL PRESS

Hachette Book Group

1290 Avenue of the Americas, New York, NY 10104

www.sealpress.com

@sealpress

Printed in the United States of America

First Edition: October 2019

Published by Seal Press, an imprint of Perseus Books, LLC,
a subsidiary of Hachette Book Group, Inc.
The Seal Press name and logo is a trademark of the Hachette Book Group.

The Hachette Speakers Bureau provides a wide range of authors for speaking events.
To find out more, go to www.hachettespeakersbureau.com or call (866) 376-6591.

The publisher is not responsible for websites (or their content)
that are not owned by the publisher.

Illustrations by Shreya Gupta

Print book interior design by Chin-Yee Lai

Library of Congress Cataloging-in-Publication Data

Names: Gore, Ariel, 1970—author.

Title: Hexing the patriarchy: 26 potions, spells, and magical elixirs
to embolden the resistance / Ariel Gore.

Description: First edition. | New York: Seal Press, [2019] | Includes index.

Identifiers: LCCN 2019013983 | ISBN 9781580058742 (hardcover: alk. paper)
| ISBN 9781580058735 (ebk.)

Subjects: LCSH: Witchcraft. | Wicca. | Charms. | Feminism. | Patriarchy.

Classification: LCC BF1571.5.W66 G67 2019 | DDC 133.4/3—dc23

LC record available at https://lccn.loc.gov/2019013983

ISBNs: 978-1-58005-874-2 (paper over board), 978-1-58005-873-5 (ebook)

LSC-C

10 9 8 7 6 5 4 3 2 1